SpringerBriefs in Law

SpringerBriefs present concise summaries of cutting-edge research and practical applications across a wide spectrum of fields. Featuring compact volumes of 50 to 125 pages, the series covers a range of content from professional to academic. Typical topics might include:

A timely report of state-of-the art analytical techniques

A bridge between new research results, as published in journal articles, and a contextual literature review

A snapshot of a hot or emerging topic

A presentation of core concepts that students must understand in order to make independent contributions

SpringerBriefs in Law showcase emerging theory, empirical research, and practical application in Law from a global author community. SpringerBriefs are characterized by fast, global electronic dissemination, standard publishing contracts, standardized manuscript preparation and formatting guidelines, and expedited production schedules.

Annelieke Mooij

Regulating the Metaverse Economy

How to Prevent Money Laundering and the Financing of Terrorism

Annelieke Mooij
Tilburg Law School
Tilburg University
Tilburg, Noord-Brabant, The Netherlands

ISSN 2192-855X   ISSN 2192-8568   (electronic)
SpringerBriefs in Law
ISBN 978-3-031-46416-4   ISBN 978-3-031-46417-1   (eBook)
https://doi.org/10.1007/978-3-031-46417-1

This work was supported by Universiteit van Tilburg
© The Editor(s) (if applicable) and The Author(s) 2024. This is an open access publication.
Open Access This book is licensed under the terms of the Creative Commons Attribution 4.0 International License (http://creativecommons.org/licenses/by/4.0/), which permits use, sharing, adaptation, distribution and reproduction in any medium or format, as long as you give appropriate credit to the original author(s) and the source, provide a link to the Creative Commons license and indicate if changes were made.
The images or other third party material in this book are included in the book's Creative Commons license, unless indicated otherwise in a credit line to the material. If material is not included in the book's Creative Commons license and your intended use is not permitted by statutory regulation or exceeds the permitted use, you will need to obtain permission directly from the copyright holder.
The use of general descriptive names, registered names, trademarks, service marks, etc. in this publication does not imply, even in the absence of a specific statement, that such names are exempt from the relevant protective laws and regulations and therefore free for general use.
The publisher, the authors, and the editors are safe to assume that the advice and information in this book are believed to be true and accurate at the date of publication. Neither the publisher nor the authors or the editors give a warranty, expressed or implied, with respect to the material contained herein or for any errors or omissions that may have been made. The publisher remains neutral with regard to jurisdictional claims in published maps and institutional affiliations.

This Springer imprint is published by the registered company Springer Nature Switzerland AG
The registered company address is: Gewerbestrasse 11, 6330 Cham, Switzerland

Paper in this product is recyclable.

Acknowledgement

I would like to thank Math Notermans of Tilburg University for his genourous aid in turning my rough sketches into the beautiful illustrations used in this book.

Contents

1	**Governing the Meta-World Finances**	1
	References	4
2	**What Is the Metaverse?**	5
	2.1 Introduction to Virtual Reality	5
	2.2 Development of Online Realities	5
	2.3 Metaverse, the Future?	7
	References	9
3	**The Virtual Currency Schemes**	11
	3.1 Introduction	11
	3.2 Virtual Currency Schemes	11
	3.3 The Metaverse	15
	3.4 The 'Real' Virtual Economy	18
	References	18
4	**Money Laundering and Financing of Terrorism via the Metaverse**	21
	4.1 Introduction	21
	4.2 The Three Phases of MLFT	22
	4.2.1 Placement	22
	4.2.2 Layering	23
	4.2.3 Integration	25
	4.3 Additional Risks Associated with the Metaverse	27
	4.3.1 Anonymity	27
	4.3.2 Jurisdiction	28
	4.3.3 Non Fungible Tokens	30
	4.4 Conclusion	32
	References	33
5	**Regulating the Technology (Placement)**	35
	5.1 Introduction: The EU Approach to the Placement of Funds	35
	5.2 Entity	36

	5.3 Custodian and Non-custodian Wallets	38
	5.4 Digital Entity	43
	5.5 Classification of Digital Personality	48
	5.6 Jurisdiction on Transactions Made to Third-Countries	52
	5.7 Smart Contracts	59
	5.8 Conclusion and Recommendations	64
	References	65
6	**Currency (Layering)**	69
	6.1 Introduction	69
	6.2 Cryptocurrencies	69
	6.3 Centralized Currency Issuers	75
	6.4 Legal Tender	77
	6.4.1 The Digital Euro	77
	6.4.2 Cryptocurrencies As Legal Tender	80
	6.5 Conclusion and Recommendations	84
	References	85
7	**Integration into the Legal Economy**	87
	7.1 Introduction	87
	7.2 Defining the Economy	88
	7.3 Value and Games	93
	7.4 Local Use	95
	7.5 Conclusion and Recommendations	97
	References	98
8	**Non-fungible Tokens and Stateless Firms**	101
	8.1 Non-fungible Tokens	101
	8.2 Stateless Firms	104
	References	107
9	**Conclusion**	109

Chapter 1
Governing the Meta-World Finances

Imagine that you live in London and are a fan of musicals. You have grown particularly fond of the musical Hamilton. As a special rendition the musical plays in New York with your favorite star singing the lead. It provides a great way for you to see the musical and catch up with your old classmate who moved to New York. Unfortunately, you live in Europe and you cannot find the time to travel to New York and back. Your option is to buy a ticket to a live screening and have a video call with your friend afterwards. Most people will agree that this is not a real alternative to seeing the musical in real life. Whilst streaming is less expensive and will save you the trouble of travelling, it does not offer the same experience. The videocall with your friend will provide you with some interaction but not on the same level as sitting next to each other at the theatre. In comes the Metaverse to provide you the immersive 3D alternative. Instead of sitting at home or in your local cinema watching the live screen in 2D, the Metaverse will allow you to buy a ticket to a virtual seat in the theatre. Your friend is sitting on the virtual seat next to you, so you both chat before the curtain call. In the break you both have a drink from your own kitchen but with the experience of being in the café of the theatre.

The development of technology is ever-continuing. The world between online and offline is getting blurred.[1] The Metaverse will bring many new experiences and increase the accessibility to these experiences. All that is needed to access the Metaverse is a device with internet access. The immersive 3D experience can be created using cardboard vr-glasses which are sold for around €15,-. In case of real deprivation, these glasses can even be fabricated at home from an old cardboard box. The possibilities of the Metaverse are endless but the Metaverse itself brings many regulatory challenges. The Metaverse can be accessed from anywhere on the planet which makes it difficult to determine which country or region has jurisdiction. The problem of jurisdiction is made even more difficult because the Metaverse is "[...]an open source decentralized, interoperable platform for programmable digital assets

---

[1] Kalpokas (2019).

© The Author(s) 2024
A. Mooij, *Regulating the Metaverse Economy*, SpringerBriefs in Law,
https://doi.org/10.1007/978-3-031-46417-1_1

and digital identities built on Substrate."[2] In non-coding language, this means that it is free and open for everyone to use. Virtual realities can be connected to the Metaverse by anyone anywhere. The code of the Metaverse is like a building platform upon which many different worlds can be built by anyone who knows how to build blocks. These worlds form a network of virtual environments.

The environments can be created and hosted by different providers and they can then be accessed at any point by anyone. It can use the real world as a template for the shared virtual reality which can be used to facilitate daily interactions.[3] The Metaverse gained fame on the 28th of October 2021 when Meta, the parent of Facebook, announced their intentions for the Metaverse. Meta intends to create meta home and meta workplace. The aim is to provide the general public with virtual reality settings designed to replace face-to-face interaction.[4] One of the potential aims of this environment is to facilitate a virtual office space whereby day-to-day office interactions will take place through virtual reality. With this potential comes a new form of virtual existence. Whilst most previous virtual realities have been created to provide an alternative world, the Metaverse would provide a virtual real-life existence. The virtual experience could cheaply facilitate a feel of real-life luxury. The hype is therefore likely to stay.

The new form of virtual existence would open up a wide array of possibilities. One can tag into the virtual office and conduct 3D business meetings. An international meeting could take place within a single virtual location. Metaverse distinguishes itself from other meeting platforms by combining a wide array of services such as communication, payment and smart contract building. The Metaverse furthermore will be provided in 3D. Due to its open source, anyone can build a reality and connect it to the Metaverse, therefore allowing a network of providers to be attached. The Metaverse will allow its users to walk through a high-end retail street, take a walk through a rainforest and close by watching a 3D football match all from their own living room. Though the Metaverse will open up new possibilities vis-à-vis the use of the internet, it also raises a series of legal questions.

These legal questions include private law matters such as the applicable law and jurisdiction over virtual contracts. Criminal law questions such as what constitutes a virtual crime. But perhaps most importantly what authority can regulate the internet? Governments aim to promote public values within their society. Whilst promoting these values they are limited to their own borders and jurisdictions. The jurisdictions are defined by physical space. Some of this space is easy to grasp such as land and some of it is a little less tangible such as water and aerial territory. Nevertheless, even the sky can be identified as what does and does not fall within a government's jurisdiction. Some of the challenges related to water and sky, such as climate change, require an international approach. Governments therefore participate in

---

[2] Metaverse (2022) Homepage. https://mvs.org/.
[3] Ondrejka (2004).
[4] Meta Press Release: The Metaverse and How We'll Build It Together – Connect 2021, 28 October 2021. Available at: https://www.youtube.com/watch?v=Uvufun6xer8.

supranational organizations. The Metaverse, however, combines national and international with a new challenge: the virtual. Whose jurisdiction applies in a virtual space? It is intangible but unlike the sky, it cannot be measured or marked. The virtual reality therefore carries the risk of becoming the new wild west. A variety of journalists have entered the Metaverse and found (sexual)harassment, discrimination and child pornography to be the order of the day.[5] This phenomenon is undesirable but has little effect in the real world and can be avoided by not entering that part of the Metaverse. The lawlessness of Metaverse also brings the risk of crimes with real-world effects such as money laundering.

Virtual reality and in particular virtual payments bring new risks with regard to money laundering and the financing of terrorism (MLFT). If left unregulated the Metaverse can provide terrorists and organized crime with new mechanisms to finance their activities. The easy solution would be to ban the Metaverse. To ban an internet product is near impossible and considering the possible advantages; is undesirable. This book will therefore consider how to regulate financial transactions through the Metaverse to prevent MLFT. It will analyze the legal framework and suggest improvements from a European Union (EU) perspective. The EU has regulated MLFT primarily through the Anti-Money Laundering Directive (AMLD). A directive requires national implementation, this book will therefore analyze national implementations for further detail.

To analyze the effectiveness and requirements of a new legal framework, Chap. 2 of this book will first describe the development of online realities and the Metaverse and the new types of transactions that can occur. Chapter 3 will discuss the different types of virtual currency schemes in relation to the physical economy. Chapter 4 will continue by examining the three phases of MLFT and the specific risks with regard to the Metaverse. This chapter will also demonstrate that there are three new risks to be added to the MLFT framework that are specific to the Metaverse. These risks are the rise of Non-Fungible Tokens, anonymity and the lack of jurisdiction. The book continues by first examining the three standard MLFT phases with regard to the Metaverse. Chapter 5 will discuss the placement phase. Chapter 6 will discuss the layering phase and Chap. 7 the integration phase. Each of these chapters will discuss the specific risks of the Metaverse and analyze whether the current EU legal framework is adept at preventing MLFT. Chapter 8 will discuss two of the new risks that are specific to the metaverse namely that of anonymity with regard to firms and the occurrence of Non-Fungible Tokens. Chapter 9 will provide a conclusion on the current legal framework and the improvements that need to be made in order to prevent MLFT through the Metaverse.

---

[5] Crawford and Smith (2022).

References

Crawford A, Smith T (2022) Metaverse app allows kids into virtual strip clubs. BBC 23 february
Kalpokas I (2019) Algorithmic governance. Politics and law in the post-human era. Palgrave Macmillan, Cham
Ondrejka C (2004) Escaping the gilded cage: user created content and building the Metaverse. New York Law School Law Rev 49(1)
Metaverse (2022) Homepage. https://mvs.org/

Open Access This chapter is licensed under the terms of the Creative Commons Attribution 4.0 International License (http://creativecommons.org/licenses/by/4.0/), which permits use, sharing, adaptation, distribution and reproduction in any medium or format, as long as you give appropriate credit to the original author(s) and the source, provide a link to the Creative Commons license and indicate if changes were made.

The images or other third party material in this chapter are included in the chapter's Creative Commons license, unless indicated otherwise in a credit line to the material. If material is not included in the chapter's Creative Commons license and your intended use is not permitted by statutory regulation or exceeds the permitted use, you will need to obtain permission directly from the copyright holder.

Chapter 2
What Is the Metaverse?

2.1 Introduction to Virtual Reality

This chapter will discuss the contours and aims of the Metaverse along with the development of virtual realities. Before discussing the legal difficulties concerning the meta-verse it is important to discuss its contours. In this discussion, an important distinction must be made between Meta and the Metaverse. The Metaverse is the 3D virtual reality that will be the central point of discussion. The Metaverse is an open-source, decentralized virtual reality that facilitates interoperability between different providers. It is the next step in the virtual reality saga, whereby virtual reality aims to take over large aspects of physical life. Meta on the other hand is the parent company of Facebook and other companies and aims to become a large provider of virtual realities connected to the Metaverse.

The discussion on how to regulate the meta-reality is not completely new. The Metaverse is in many ways comparable to other virtual realities. There are various developments of virtual worlds. The most popular and well-known virtual worlds are perhaps those offered through games. The development of games is complex. There are multiple layers and levels of development.[1] For the purposes of regulating the economy of the Metaverse, it is only necessary to examine three earlier developments.

2.2 Development of Online Realities

The first is the offline virtual world. This world was developed through a variety of games, most famously, Super Mario. The user would buy the gaming software, install it on a device and the user could then experience a virtual reality. This reality

---
[1] Ivory (2016), pp. 1–2.

however was limited to one user who was alone in the virtual reality. A similar development was the Sims a virtual game whereby users would play in a simulated real-life world. This development is the first leading to virtual realities based upon a real-world environment. With the development of the internet, the same type of gaming content became available online. The online virtual worlds allowed multiple players to connect and play within the same virtual world. These are called the Massive Multi-player Online games (MMO).

The MMO games form the second development in the gaming development. Unlike offline games, the MMOs allow interaction and cooperation between different players. The first graphical MMO in existence was Neverwinter Nights[2] a role-playing game based upon the board game Dungeons and Dragons. The MMOs currently include famous gaming worlds such as World of Warcraft (WoW) and Runescape. WoW at its height had an estimated amount of 7.2million users and currently has around 1.1million.[3] These games are characterized by an online virtual world in which the players emerge themselves. Unlike the offline games, users can interact in the virtual environment. The users can earn and buy gold from the platform provider and use it to buy virtual assets. This game is closely related to the third development that of MMOs with economies with a link to the real economy.

The third development is that of MMOs with a link to the economy outside the gaming industry. The most famous of these games was Second Life, a game based upon simulating the real world. Second Life in 2020 had an estimated user number of 600.000.[4] Whilst currently past its peak, the platform had 36 million accounts created and a daily transaction rate of 1.2 million dollars.[5] There are two important differences between Second Life and the earlier MMOs. The first is the intention which is that of a simulation based upon the real world. The second is that of the economy in Second Life. Users can purchase coins with dollars but also earn them by working for another user or by operating a shop. They can furthermore exchange their virtual coins for fiat currency. This exchange created a link between the real economy and the virtual economy. There are several similarities between the Metaverse and Second Life.

Similar to Second Life users of the Metaverse can communicate and trade with each other. The platform allows the users to exchange virtual goods and services. The aim of the Metaverse, like Second Life, is to provide a reality based on real life. However, unlike Second Life the Metaverse will allow users to emerge in the environment using virtual reality glasses. Thus whilst walking through their own homes users can feel like they are in their work environments and meet other

---

[2] Ibid, p. 12.
[3] MMO Populations. World of Warcraft Stats. Available at: https://mmo-population.com/r/wow/stats.
[4] Ibid.
[5] Linden Lab Press Release: Infographic: 10 years of second life. Available at: https://www.lindenlab.com/releases/infographic-10-years-of-second-life.

colleagues. The second large difference between Second Life and the Metaverse is interoperability. Due to its open-source code, the Metaverse will be able to connect to virtual environments provided by other companies. Second Life on the other hand was a closed virtual environment provided by a single source. To explain it in less technical terms, consider Legos.

2.3 Metaverse, the Future?

Virtual reality such as Second Life can be compared to a world created by Legos. The world is provided by one company (Lego) which has created the world, decorations and characters. Whilst the same company can create different themes and different worlds, these are separated into different boxes. And whilst the Lego worlds are sold and offered throughout the world, the company is located in a small number of jurisdictions. Therefore the themes can be played throughout the world but in case there is an issue consumers can easily establish the applicable legal regime. The interesting thing about Legos is that you can connect the blocks. You could build one room and then build the next and attach it. Before Lego lost its patent only Lego created the specific blocks that could be connected, now these blocks are created by a number of providers. These worlds can be accessed from the Lego rooms or through their own door. When entering the other room, one leaves the world offered by Lego and enters one offered by a competitor. And whilst Lego used to create the entire universe, including decorations and characters, now these can be designed by competitors. This means that a company specialising in the creation of avatars might be providing the characters walking throughout the world. Another company can create the art hanging on the walls, or even individuals can make and hang up their own art. Thus creating a complex mix of different providers. Metaverse is like these Lego-built rooms but after Lego lost its patent. All environments are built upon the same baseplate (source code) but built by different providers. Adding to the mix of complexity is the strange jurisdiction. When Lego sells its products through a store, it generally falls under the jurisdiction of the store it sells through, there are fewer such clarities in virtual reality. Thus allowing for an almost infinite amount of jurisdictions to be part of the same virtual environment. Metaverse, however, is different from previous online environments in various ways.

The previous environments were purposed for a single function: entertainment. Whilst the gaming industry is a large business, only a few games remain successful for a long period of time. Virtual reality, however, is not the same as a game. Whilst virtual reality has its origins in gaming it has often different objectives. Second Life for example was not described as a game by its designers. It is a virtual environment where users can explore without gaming obstacles or objectives. Though its popularity decreased slightly, Second Life still had a $600 GDP in 2021.[6] A virtual reality

---

[6] Galov (2023).

that is not perse designed as a game whereby obstacles should be overcome can generate long-term revenue. The Metaverse is considered more likely to be successful. As it encompasses various objectives.

The Metaverse can offer entertainment such as attending virtual concerts, plays or festivals. Such as the musical example given in the introduction of this book. However, the Metaverse can offer a wider variety of services. Such as online shopping whereby an avatar that looks exactly like its user can try on various items of clothing. These virtual dressing rooms can mimic the experience of trying on clothing but without the hassle of having to physically change outfits.[7] This experience is made possible by what is described as the three illusions of virtual reality. Virtual reality provides the user with three illusions: place, embodiment and plausibility.[8] The user will see the virtual surroundings of a dressing room through the mobile device. This illusion is strengthened by the ability of the Metaverse to respond interactively.[9] The clothing can furthermore be programmed to fall as it would in real life and respond to the behaviour of the user. A skirt could digitally swirl in response to the user spinning through its own physical environment. The Metaverse thus facilitates online shopping by mimicking the physical benefits of examining goods with the easy accessibility of virtual reality. In addition to facilitating the online purchase of physical goods, the Metaverse will generate its own economy. The ownership of digital goods is expected to increase. As seen in the previous section, in earlier game environments the ownership of virtual items generates real value. Previous virtual realities differ from the Metaverse in an important aspect: Non-Fungible Tokens (NFTs). These are digital certificates of ownership that digitally guarantee a sense of unique ownership. The NFTs are considered to be the fourth illusion. These NFTs provide the illusion of digital ownership.[10] They are mined on a blockchain and cannot be replicated. Through the use of NFTs digital scarcity is created. Scarcity is the foundation of the economy, yet it was not present before the introduction of blockchain technology.[11] The Metaverse therefore offers new opportunities to create a virtual economy. With virtual pieces of art that sell for high value. The most famous example of this is likely the Bored Ape virtual imagery which ranges in price from $63,000 to $13 million.[12]

In addition to generating a new type of economy, the Metaverse is also adaptable to generate new types of learning environments.[13] The Metaverse can be used to provide a realistic type of training environment for vocational training. Such as providing a realistic environment for police officers or giving aspiring surgeons the

---

[7] Shams (2023).
[8] Ruco (2023), pp. 48–49.
[9] Ibid.
[10] Ibid, p. 49.
[11] Ibid, pp. 49–50.
[12] As on offer on OpenSea on 10 july 2023.
[13] Hwang and Chien (2022).

possibility to practice in a realistic operating theatre. Metaverse applications can help students develop their soft skills in simulated environments.[14] The Metaverse can furthermore be used in high school history classes to experience the Stone Age. Or to provide children with a classroom experience during a pandemic. Metaverse can facilitate attendance to training courses across the globe at low costs. A student from a developing nation could attend university lectures without having to travel. The university providing the course does not need additional physical space for the student. The additional costs of receiving that student are relatively low. In combination with AI, the Metaverse can be used to generate personal lesson plans for students. This could help provide a more tailored learning approach for the individual students.[15] The potential educational opportunities of the Metaverse are large.

In addition to educational opportunities, the Metaverse can help provide tools for public bodies. Tools can be generated for urban planning.[16] Whereby the designer, potential users and neighbours can virtually walk through the planned urban development. Similarly, tools can be generated for traffic planning. Or the design of a public facility such as a new sports centre or community building.

These are just a few of the potential applications of the Metaverse. The limitless opportunities make it that it is expected that VR and AR will increase global GDP by $1.5 trillion in 2030.[17] The Metaverse is a large part of the VR experience. The Metaverse market is expected to reach $1.35 billion by 2025.[18] Thus demonstrating the big expectations of companies and their willingness to enter the Metaverse.

The combination of different virtual world providers makes the legal governing of Metaverse more complex. This complexity is enhanced when considering some of the latest developments in financial technology such as cryptocurrency. The legislation will therefore have to take into consideration that there are different structural designs of transactions. However, before analyzing the different legislative conundrums the next section will first describe the potential payment structures available in the Metaverse.

References

Galov N (2023) '18 second life facts in 2023: what it means to live in a Virtual World', webtribunal (6 maart)
Hwang G-J, Chien S-Y (2022) Definition, roles and potential research issues of the metaverse in education: an artificial intelligence perspective. Comp Edu Artif Intelligence 3:100082
Ivory JD (2016) A brief history of video games. In: Kowert TQR (ed) The video game debate. Unravelling the psychological effects of digital games. Routledge, London

---

[14] Sabtu (2023).
[15] Ibid.
[16] Kemeç (2023).
[17] Rijmenam (2022), p. 33.
[18] Walbank (2023). Top 10 companies investing in the metaverse in 2023. Mobile Magazine.

Kemeç A (2023) Metaverse applications as a tool in urban policy design. In: Anshari M, Syafrudin U, Alfian G (eds) Metaverse applications for new business models and disruptive innovation. IGI Global, Hershey

Rijmenam M (2022) Step into the Metaverse. How the immersive internet will unlock a trillion-dollar social economy. Wiley, Hoboken

Ruco A (2023) The fourth illusion: how a new economy of consumption is being created in the Metaverse. In: Lai PC (ed) Strategies and opportunities for technology in the metaverse world. IGI Global, Hershey

Sabtu M (2023) Metaverse and soft skills development through video games. In: Anshari M, Syafrudin U, Alfian G (eds) Metaverse applications for new business models and disruptive innovation. IGI Global, Hershey

Shams MY, Elzeki OM, Marie HS (2023) Towards 3D virtual dressing room based user-friendly metaverse strategy. In: Hassanien AE, Darwish A, Torky M (eds) The future of Metaverse in the virtual era and physical world. Springer, Cham

Walbank (2023) Top 10 companies investing in the metaverse in 2023. Mobile Magazine

Open Access This chapter is licensed under the terms of the Creative Commons Attribution 4.0 International License (http://creativecommons.org/licenses/by/4.0/), which permits use, sharing, adaptation, distribution and reproduction in any medium or format, as long as you give appropriate credit to the original author(s) and the source, provide a link to the Creative Commons license and indicate if changes were made.

The images or other third party material in this chapter are included in the chapter's Creative Commons license, unless indicated otherwise in a credit line to the material. If material is not included in the chapter's Creative Commons license and your intended use is not permitted by statutory regulation or exceeds the permitted use, you will need to obtain permission directly from the copyright holder.

Chapter 3
The Virtual Currency Schemes

3.1 Introduction

Due to its interoperability, the Metaverse will provide a different virtual economy than currently in existence. The Metaverse could combine the convenience of staying at home with daily (office) interactions.[1] The potential applications of this type of virtual reality are therefore endless. In particular, it is likely the Metaverse will facilitate a variety of economic transactions. Before entering the debate on whether the current legislation can govern the Metaverse, it is important to distinguish between different virtual currency systems. The dissection of the different currency systems will enable the next chapter to analyze the risks and legal framework necessary. This dissection will be done according to the developments of the virtual worlds as described in the previous section. The systems will be described according to a virtual currency classification developed by the European Central Bank (ECB).

3.2 Virtual Currency Schemes

The ECB provides three different types of virtual currency definitions.[2] These definitions are established in the contours of examining monetary policy and do not form legal definitions. They are however practically useful in defining the different types of virtual currency and their respective MLFT risks. The first virtual currency scheme considered by the ECB is a "closed virtual currency". This type of

---

[1] Meta Press Release: The Metaverse and How We'll Build It Together – Connect 2021, 28 October 2021. Available at: https://www.youtube.com/watch?v=Uvufun6xer8.
[2] European Central Bank (2012).

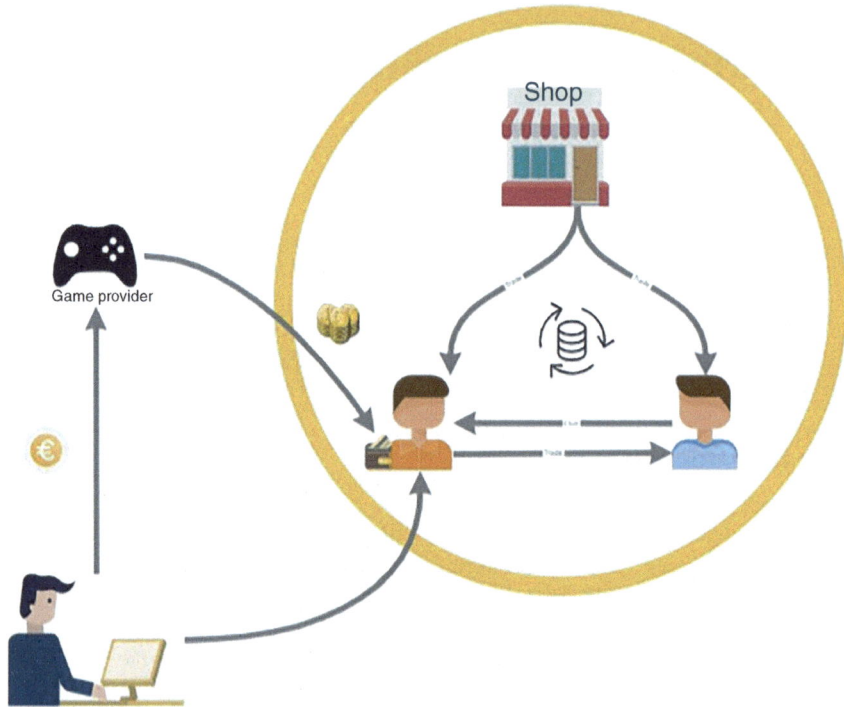

Fig. 3.1 Uni-directional flow

scheme does not have a connection to the real world.[3] Under this type of scheme, the currency cannot be bought or sold and is given based on a game subscription or in-game reward. This type of currency is best compared to the offline games. These types of schemes have no risk of MLFT and will not be given any further attention.

The second scheme is described as a "uni-directional flow". Within a virtual reality based upon a uni-directional flow, the virtual currency can be bought with fiat currency. The virtual currency can then only be spent within a single virtual reality.[4] These schemes are often found in games whereby the player is able to purchase the in-game currency. This currency can then only be used to buy virtual in-game items and quests. Most MMO games are based on this concept.

Figure 3.1 shows a closed system currency and economy. The virtual currency cannot be used to purchase real-life goods, its redemption rate is therefore limited. The currency furthermore cannot be traded for fiat currency and there is only one provider of the virtual economy. The regulation of this economy can therefore be done by simply regulating the providers. This system is however the most simple

---

[3] Ibid, p. 15.
[4] Ibid.

3.2 Virtual Currency Schemes

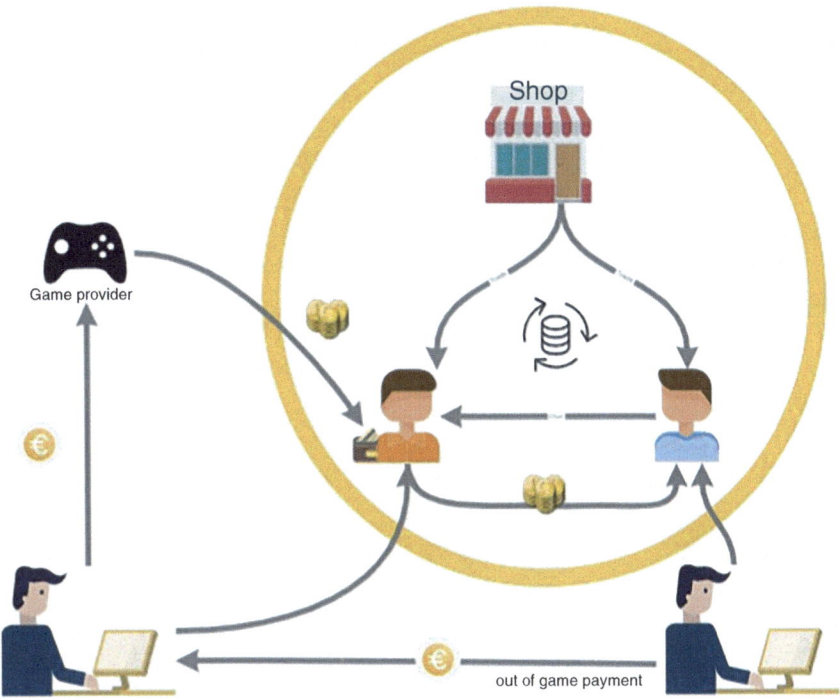

Fig. 3.2 Virtual currency with unintended ties to real economy

virtual economy currently in existence. More complicated is the third scheme identified by the ECB.

This scheme provides a "bi-directional flow" meaning that the currency can be purchased and sold through the real economy.[5] There are two different types of virtual currency schemes with a bi-directional flow. Staying with the example of WoW, officially the trade in WoW currency outside of the official platform is prohibited.[6] Users are not allowed to buy currency other than through the platform provider.

There is, however, a lively black market. The black market as indicated by Fig. 3.2 provides ties to the real economy. It is therefore possible for players to gather or buy virtual currency which they can transfer to other players or convert to fiat currency. This type of currency scheme creates a potential for conducting MLFT. The currency acquisition requires little effort as it can be bought from the gaming platform. It can then be transferred to another player and converted into fiat currency. It is furthermore difficult to regulate as it is not the virtual reality provider that created or supervises this market. This system should therefore be considered as a

---

[5] Ibid.
[6] Article C.iii of the Blizzard end-user license agreement.

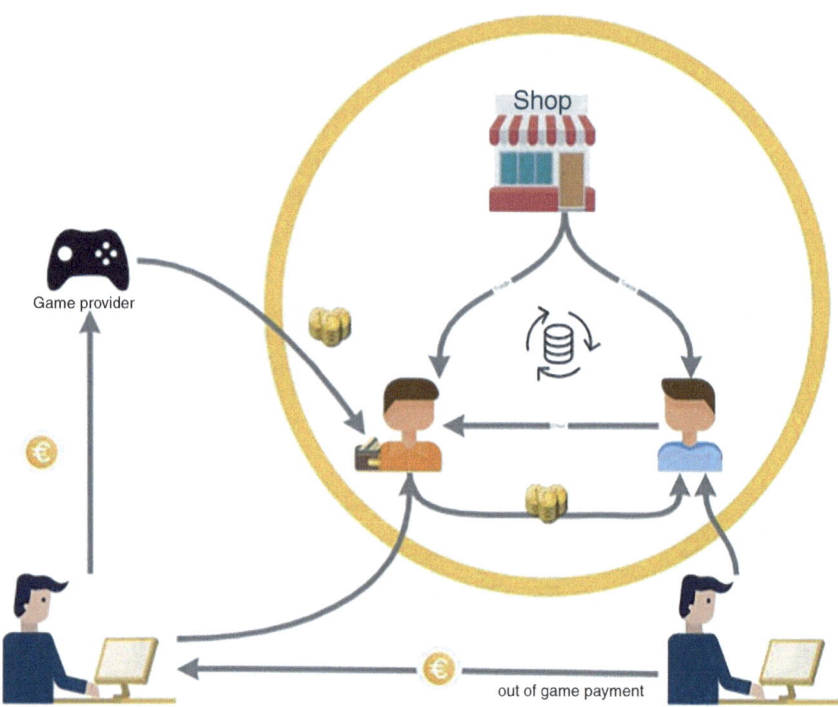

Fig. 3.3 Virtual currency with intended ties to real economy

currency with an unintentional bi-directional flow. These systems are particularly vulnerable to MLFT because of the lack of supervision. Research found that the game Fortnite was used frequently for MLFT purposes.[7] Another research indicated that a two-month eBay surveillance had produced 53,000 signals of money laundering.[8] Black markets with MMO games should therefore be considered of high MLFT risk.[9] The black markets are furthermore more difficult to regulate than the intended bi-directional flow designs.

Figure 3.3 has an intended flow between the currency used on its platform and fiat currency. The users can buy and sell currency to the platform provider, trade with each other and buy virtual items in different shops. This virtual reality is more complex than that of most MMOs. Users can operate shops and earn currency through the platform. Thus making it more difficult to discover potential money laundering. However, as only the provider exchanges the currency it is easier to regulate. As it only requires the regulation of a single provider. However, a potential black market can still arise which would be a likely source of MLFT.

---

[7] Cuthbertson (2019).
[8] Crijns (2019).
[9] Richet (2013).

The black market would be a serious indicator for MLFT. The only way to make the black market economically attractive is by selling the virtual currency against a lower fiat currency rate. Thus providing a loss to the trader on the black market. Leaving aside altruistic reasons, the main motivator for taking a loss on the black market is to avoid official or monitored channels. Thus the black market provides a serious indication that the traders have illicit motivations. The transactions occur partially between characters online and payment takes place offline. Thus regulation and governance are not unlike that in the physical world. With the general challenges of monitoring MLFT.

The current design of online environments has therefore led to three distinct currency schemes. The schemes with a bi-directional flow carry the most risk of MLFT. In particular when the bi-directional flow is left unsupervised. The Metaverse has payment options built into the platform and will therefore become a reality with a bi-directional flow. The economy and payment infrastructure within the Metaverse will be more complex than a simple bi-directional flow. Unlike the previously discussed schemes, the Metaverse will incorporate multiple coins, payment services and exchange opportunities.

3.3 The Metaverse

The Metaverse is interoperable with various platforms. That means that the eventual reality of the Metaverse will be highly complex. This section will examine the currency scheme from the simplest to the most complex version. The focus will be to identify the possible transactions, currency used and the providers involved. The Metaverse will primarily contain the bi-directional flow virtual currency scheme identified by the ECB. Yet it is not accurate to speak in terms of uni and bi-directional flows. The bi-directional flow virtual schemes identified by the ECB are only adapted to the first scenario that will be discussed. This research has therefore decided to generate its own terminology. This terminology will be based on the relationships that will be in existence.

The first version of the Metaverse that will be examined is one whereby the whole universe is regulated by a single provider. The example is given in Fig. 3.4. For this example, this research has chosen to use the Metaverse provider. In this scenario, the transactions are made between the participants through virtual avatars created by Metaverse. The avatars use the digital wallet also provided through the same provider. The currency used for payment between the participants is also provided by the same provider. The object sold and Non-Fungible Token (NFT) is also created through the Metaverse. From a regulatory perspective, this scenario is the simplest to govern. There is only one party to govern. This scenario will be considered a 'single party Metaverse'. Unfortunately, this scenario is the least likely to occur most frequently. As stated before the Metaverse allows for interoperability. Thus making it more likely that the virtual transactions occur through different providers.

Fig. 3.4 Metaverse room fully operated by a single provider

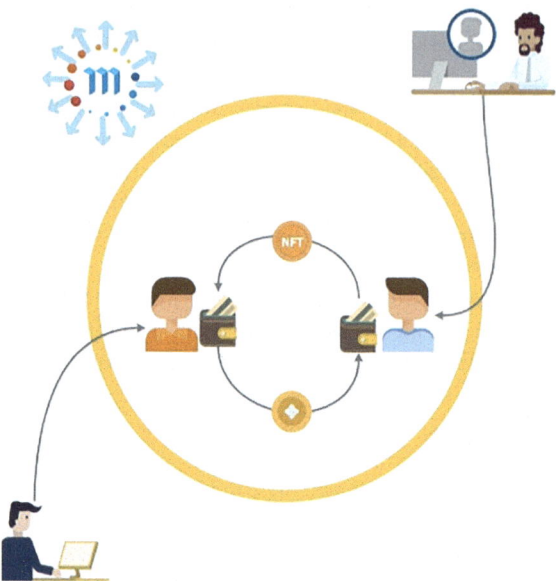

A reality provided by a provider different from the provider of the wallets would constitute a dual-party Metaverse. Though such an environment would technically not be too difficult to govern, it gains complexity. The complexity could be increased when more providers are added to form a multi-party party Metaverse. This system becomes more complex when considering that not all transactions and services remain within the same room or even within the Metaverse.

The next scenario increases the complexity by adding a third-party, outside of the first room to deliver a service inside the virtual reality (Fig. 3.5). This could be a virtual service such as a translator or a virtual object such as a virtual watch. These situations demonstrate the increase in complexity. Furthermore as demonstrated the same wallet and currency can be used inside the Metaverse and outside. The wallets can purchase goods online which are either virtual or physical. These transactions can be labelled as "third-party transactions". These types of structures can be continued to increasing complexity.

Figure 3.6 provides a good overview of the difficulties that will be associated with regulating and governing the Metaverse. There are different providers of realities, and payment structures coming together in a web of interactions. Before identifying the exact risks. There is one more complexity that needs to be discussed: the real economy of the Metaverse.

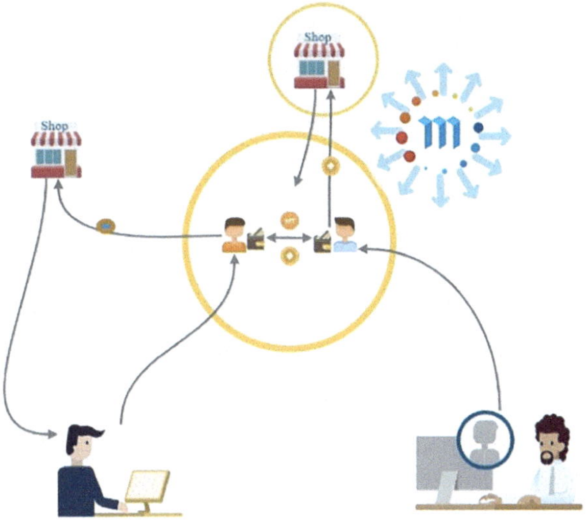

3.3 The Metaverse

Fig. 3.5 Metaverse reality with multiple parties and external transactions

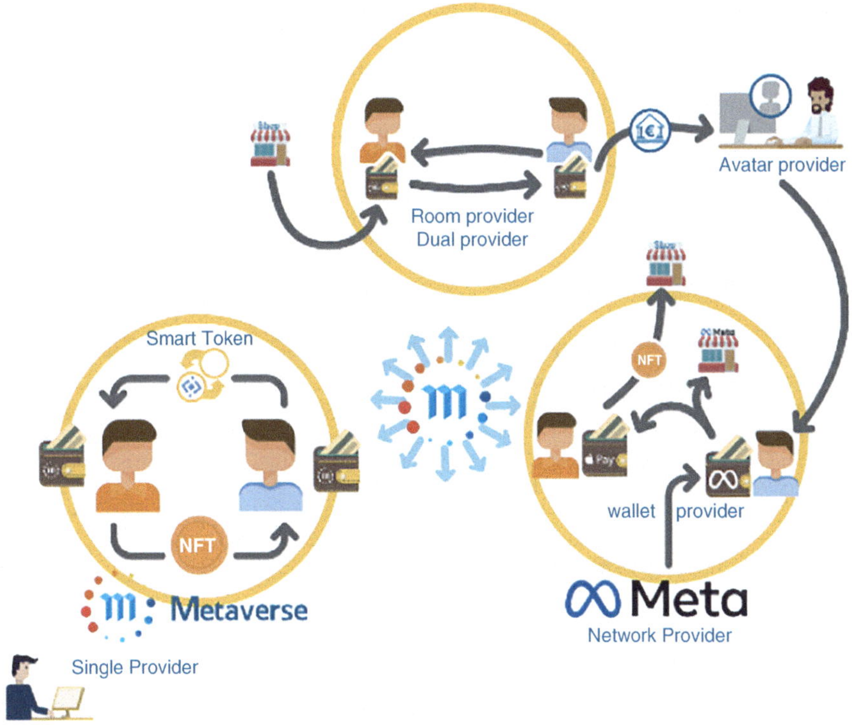

Fig. 3.6 Complex metaverse world

3.4 The 'Real' Virtual Economy

The Metaverse potentially offers another complexity compared to earlier versions of virtual realities and that is the 'real' value of virtual items. In earlier virtual realities the virtual goods had no value outside the providing virtual reality. The reason for this lack of value is that virtual goods cannot be transferred to or enjoyed in the real world.

The Metaverse will allow for virtual shopping whereby physical products are shipped to the buyer's home address. However, the Metaverse will also introduce the enjoyment of virtual goods in real life. Mark Zuckerberg CEO of Meta, however, explains this lack of real enjoyment might change in the future. In his opinion, a hologram TV will replace the physical TV in our homes.[10] Continuing in this line of possibilities the art on our walls might become virtual rather than physical. The need for physical goods therefore might decrease and virtual items gain in value. There are however items that cannot be replaced by virtual objects. In order to comfortably watch TV, a physical chair or couch will still be needed. Similarly, it will be difficult to satisfy one's hunger with virtual food. The real economy however should not be limited to the physical realm, as the Metaverse has the potential to provide enjoyment of virtual assets.

The Metaverse economy would therefore result in a highly complex system that has links with the physical and virtual economy but with little need for central banks and regulated financial services. Considering this new reality that society is facing the question is where the risks of MLFT are.

References

Crijns D (2019) Money laundering with Fortnite. Anti Money Laundering Centre Rijksoverheid. https://www.amlc.eu/money-laundering-with-fortnite/

Cuthbertson A (13 January 2019) How children playing Fortnite are helping to fuel organised crime. The Independent

European Central Bank (2012) Virtual Currency Schemes. Frankfurt. https://www.ecb.europa.eu/pub/pdf/other/virtualcurrencyschemes201210en.pdf

Richet J (2013) Laundering money online: a review of cybercriminals' methods', Tools and Resources for Anti-Corruption Knowledge – June, 01, 2013 – United Nations Office on Drugs and Crime (UNODC)

---

[10] Meta Press Release: The Metaverse and How We'll Build It Together – Connect 2021, 28 October 2021. Available at: https://www.youtube.com/watch?v=Uvufun6xer8.

References

Open Access This chapter is licensed under the terms of the Creative Commons Attribution 4.0 International License (http://creativecommons.org/licenses/by/4.0/), which permits use, sharing, adaptation, distribution and reproduction in any medium or format, as long as you give appropriate credit to the original author(s) and the source, provide a link to the Creative Commons license and indicate if changes were made.

The images or other third party material in this chapter are included in the chapter's Creative Commons license, unless indicated otherwise in a credit line to the material. If material is not included in the chapter's Creative Commons license and your intended use is not permitted by statutory regulation or exceeds the permitted use, you will need to obtain permission directly from the copyright holder.

Chapter 4
Money Laundering and Financing of Terrorism via the Metaverse

4.1 Introduction

In the days when cash was the predominant form of currency, MLFT required some form of physical transfer. The physical transfer depended on nearness, smuggling and/or money mules. Digital currency has facilitated remote payments. The introduction of remote payments evolved the face of MLFT from physical nearness to an emphasis on suspicious bank transactions. The introduction of virtual and immersive internet will induce the next evolution of MLFT. This chapter will discuss the risks associated with virtual reality and MLFT. The aim of this risk assessment is to provide a framework for regulatory needs.

It is not possible to provide accurate numbers on the volume of MLFT. The IMF estimates that on an annual basis, the amount of money laundered is between 2 and 5% of the global GDP.[1] Money laundering is traditionally conducted through three stages. These stages are placement, layering and integration.[2] Concerning virtual money laundering, the same stages can be identified.[3] These three stages will be discussed first. This chapter will then continue by discussing the differences between virtual and physical MLFT concerning risk. The chapter will close with a conclusion that provides the specific risks unique to the Metaverse. These risks will be used in the next chapters to analyze the legal framework.

---

[1] Weeks-Brown (2018), p. 44.
[2] Van den Broek (2015), p. 1.
[3] Nagy and Mezei (2016), p. 146.

4.2 The Three Phases of MLFT

4.2.1 Placement

The first is the placement of goods in an institution or through the purchase of an asset. The storage of virtual currency is through a virtual wallet (further: wallet). The wallet for virtual currencies can be offered in attachment to the avatar, a separate wallet provider or a payment system connected to the virtual room. Once the Metaverse is developed, additional technologies will likely be developed offering new payment solutions. A legislative framework therefore has to be broad enough to incorporate all wallets that allow for funds to enter the Metaverse. It furthermore has to be flexible enough to incorporate new technologies. Similarly, various types of currency can be distinguished within the Metaverse. Such as cryptocurrency, smart coins and centralized currency—the same therefore applies to currency inclusion. The first Metaverse-related risk is therefore the broad spectrum of wallets and currency available. In particular, because the accessibility of wallets facilitates a technology called smurfing.

Small amounts of money generally raise less suspicion than large transfers. To avoid detection money launderers opt for a placement technique called 'smurfing'.[4] Smurfing is a process whereby small amounts of money are placed into the system. There are two types of smurfing techniques. The first is from multiple sources through one institution into multiple outlets. The second is placing small sums through multiple institutions into one outlet.[5] The advantage of smurfing techniques is that the small amounts often go unnoticed. The disadvantage of this technique was the intensity of bringing in a large number of small amounts. The use of smurfing is fairly easy to conduct through virtual financial institutions, in particular in combination with anonymous MMO accounts.[6] The virtual accounts can be created anonymously and generally without paperwork.[7] The placing of funds into the system is largely an automated process. This process can be carried out by robots or through self-executing smart contracts.[8] Virtual reality facilitates the process of smurfing. The lack of regulation and supervision within the Metaverse may generate a second case of Liberty Reserve.

The organization 'Liberty Reserve' conducted its transactions without customer verification.[9] It furthermore did not accept transactions with registered financial institutions and its customers used a cryptocurrency.[10] It acted in any form of customer due diligence that is expected of regulated financial institutes. The result

---

[4] Irwin and Choo (2012), pp. 94–95.
[5] Dong et al. (2021), p. 173.
[6] Irwin and Choo (2012), p. 64.
[7] Keene (2012), pp. 32–33.
[8] Dupuis and Gleason (2022), p. 10.
[9] Mabunda (2018).
[10] Ibid.

was a large amount of money from criminal origins being moved. The 'bank' itself was established in Costa Rica and became known as the bank of the underworld.[11] The Liberty Reserve exemplifies the risks of unregulated institutes. Furthermore, the cryptocurrency used for transactions was largely anonymous, thus amplifying the attractiveness for criminals.

The risk of placement is therefore amplified when considering virtual currencies. This risk increases even further in the Metaverse. Smurfing used to be intensive as it required a lot of small amounts to be placed. This intensity can be reduced through the use of robots and smart contracts. The Metaverse will "[allow] *anyone to build smart contracts and deploy them to the Metaverse chain, using tools like MetaMask, Remix, and Truffle. Smart contracts will be compatible through the provided support for Solidity as well as for anything that compiles to EVM bytecode.*"[12] The use of smart contracts is built into the system, which can be designed and operated by anyone. Thus increasing the risk of smurfing. The placement of illegal proceeds into the Metaverse is fairly easy. Placing low amounts of money into the system is not illegal, but can indicate MLFT. Regulation and supervision is therefore of paramount importance.

4.2.2 Layering

The second stage of MLFT is to hide the criminal origin of the good through layering. During this process, false proof of origin is created. With physical goods, this would include creating false paperwork and other tedious processes. Virtual currencies have made this process much easier. Cryptocurrencies can be transferred fast, across borders and with little need for exchange or intermediary services.[13] The speed of blockchain transactions is largely due to the automized process. Unlike financial institutions a blockchain does not clear transactions, thus providing speed but through reduction of a governance layer. The transaction records are recorded on a blockchain but the encryption keys are private. And little to no private information has to be released in order to conduct a transaction over the blockchain.[14] The reduction of the clearing layer has made cryptocurrencies a popular alternative to bank transfers. The anonymity aids criminal activities and the reduction of official institutions greatly reduces the supervision. The blockchain has a clear record of all transactions but linking these transactions to a person is difficult.[15]

---

[11] Liberty Reserve a 'black-market bank', BBC News 29 May 2013, available on https://www.youtube.com/watch?v=Fh3WSFcACNE.

[12] Metaverse (2022) Homepage. https://mvs.org/.

[13] Mbiyavanga (2019), p. 6.

[14] Albrecht and Duffin (2019), p. 213.

[15] Dyntu and Dykyi (2018), pp. 75–81.

It furthermore takes very little effort to create a new wallet to store the currencies. Thus facilitating layering through various wallets owned by a single individual. In addition, criminals can make use of "mixing" services. These are services that mix cryptocurrencies with other currencies through random transactions. Thereby concealing the origins of the currency.[16] In addition to mixing services, cryptocurrency users can initiate payments via TOR networks. These networks direct traffic through several relays, thereby hiding the origin of the transaction.[17] By hiding the origin of the transaction it becomes particularly difficult to estimate risks. Similarly, a person can own several wallets and quickly move the cryptocurrency from one wallet to another.[18] Legislation aiming to prevent layering should therefore aim to prevent anonymizing transactions.[19] In addition to decentralized payment systems, the Metaverse will likely also offer home to centralized virtual currencies.

Centralized virtual currencies are those that are offered and governed by a single platform. When considering centralized virtual currencies the regulation of layering is slightly easier. Centralized currencies can be largely regulated through the provider. Nevertheless, even centralized currencies can be transferred and layered quickly. Similarly, the currency that Facebook (now Meta) was planning to introduce, would allow transactions with multiple stores. These stores would however still be connected to the offering platform, in this case, Facebook. Regulating the provider is slightly easier but should not be considered a snake-oil cure. Currencies can be monitored for transaction rate and/or geographic holder movement. However, this does not provide a watertight system of governance. The main contribution would be that tokens could be followed in addition to currencies going in and out of a wallet. Think of it as adding GPS tracker systems to individual cash notes. These could flare up when passed very rapidly or across various borders. Whilst a useful addition in the fight against MLFT it would lose its function if the storage facilities were not monitored.

Whilst therefore made easier to regulate, transactions can still occur rapidly and privacy concerns may prevent monitoring every transaction. The legislative framework would therefore have to entail a supervisory element that allows monitoring without violation of privacy. Furthermore, there is a risk of black market exchange. Such exchange was identified as the main process of MLFT through gaming websites. This concerned a process of integration into the legal economy which will be discussed in the next paragraphs.

---

[16] Mbiyavanga (2019), p. 6.
[17] Dyntu and Dykyi (2018), pp. 75–81.
[18] Ibid.
[19] See to that effect Dyntu and Dykyi (2018), p. 79.

4.2.3 Integration

The third phase of MLFT is where the good goes through the process of integration into the legal economy.[20] This is an interesting issue that needs discussion. The integration into the legal economy through virtual currency often requires the exchange of fiat currency. A legislative framework therefore has to regulate the exchange of virtual currency into fiat currency. The regulation of formal exchanges, however, is not enough. Technically speaking a closed virtual currency system would pose less risk because there is no integration into the legal economy.[21] However, there are three issues with this theory. The first is that of black markets, the second is the concept of legal economy and the third is the redemption value of the currencies.

Gaming platforms theoretically posed little MLFT risks as they were a closed virtual currency system. However, large MLFT practices have been discovered to have occurred through gaming sites. The virtual currencies of gaming platforms had little to no value. Virtual objects have no value for either terrorists or crime syndicates. Therefore the virtual currency had to be exchanged into fiat currency or cryptocurrencies. Such an exchange is in most cases in violation of the intellectual property rights of the gaming platform. The intellectual property rights violation, however, did not prevent MLFT from occurring through closed virtual currency platforms. The MLFT was conducted through gaming sites, developed through the black market possibility of fiat exchanges. With the increase of exchange opportunities comes the increase in MLFT.

In 2012 Stokes concluded that the MLFT occurring through this type of gaming sites was limited.[22] A year later the same type of MLFT network was considered threatening.[23] In 2019 the Independent discovered that the MLFT through a game called 'Fortnite' was significant.[24] The main accomplices that aided in the integration of money into the legal economy were minors. The trade of V-Bucks[25] was sold globally to normal players (the minors) through both ordinary social media such as Instagram and Twitter and illegal trading sites through the dark web.[26] Whilst the sale of virtual items was temporarily banned by eBay,[27] it is not difficult to transfer virtual currency into fiat currency. There are companies that trade in these currencies, despite it usually violating intellectual property. Supervision of these games and trading companies is virtually non-existent.[28] Closed currencies in the

---

[20] Van den Broek (2015).
[21] Vandezande (2017), pp. 341–342.
[22] Stokes (2012).
[23] Richet (2013).
[24] Cuthbertson (2019).
[25] The currency used in the game Fortnite.
[26] Cuthbertson (2019).
[27] Terdiman (2007).
[28] Mooij (2022a, b).

Metaverse can generate black markets if their value is considered high. The legal framework therefore has to include closed currency schemes in the supervision against MLFT, to prevent black markets from occurring. This leads to the second question, namely what constitutes the legal economy.

The Metaverse might change the concept of integration completely. Lin's research indicates that virtual consumption might replace part of physical consumption.[29] Consumers can generate satisfaction from the consumption of virtual items, often similar to their consumption of physical items.[30] If simple activities such as watching television transcend into the Metaverse, the need for physical goods decreases. Thereby the need for integration into the physical legal economy decreases. The goods could be bought and consumed virtually. Arguably there is still a process of integration into the legal economy of the Metaverse. However, if the Metaverse economy is not regulated and actively supervised it would not constitute a legal economy as per the definition of MLFT. This is particularly difficult for the legislation to take into consideration. As discussed earlier certain types of goods will still be consumed physically such as a couch and a car. A legislative approach to MLFT therefore has to consider that the integration into the legal economy has changed. The integration has changed from exclusively the conversion of cryptocurrency to fiat currency to include the conversion of cryptocurrency to virtual assets. In addition, there is the question as to the redemption possibilities for physical assets. Whereby goods are bought in a virtual space and sent to the buyer's physical address. This leads to the last integration question, that of redemption.

Closed currency schemes can generate black markets that facilitate MLFT or provide their own level of redemption. A closed scheme can pose a risk to MLFT when the redemption scope is increased. A loyalty programme such as air miles with a large redemption scope can be an attractive currency. The risk of a scheme therefore should not be based solely on the possibility of exchanging the currency to fiat currency. Important risk factors are the possibility of purchasing awards, international transaction possibility and a potential unregulated market.[31] In the earlier mentioned Liberty Reserve case customers could wire currency or spend it in shops that accepted the Liberty Reserve currency. When a virtual currency is increasingly accepted by sellers, the need for conversion decreases. El Salvador has currently made Bitcoin a legal tender,[32] indicating the potential rise in acceptance of cryptocurrency.[33] The increased acceptance of cryptocurrency reduces the need to convert to fiat currency. In particular, the Metaverse provides this risk. Virtual realities can be created to mimic shopping streets. These streets could either accept cryptocurrency or even create their own coins. The shops located on these streets can send physical goods to the buyer. This possibility is increased by new technological

---

[29] Bray and Konsynski (2006), pp. 113–114.
[30] Ibid.
[31] Dostov and Shust (2014), p. 393.
[32] Renteria et al. (2021).
[33] El Salvador's decision to use Bitcoin as legal tender, however, is controversial.

developments in the area of virtual fitting. It is now possible to generate an avatar based on body measurements or a body scan and try on an item of clothing. Virtual reality can show the potential customer how the item fits and falls around the body without the need to physically try it. The only challenge at present is the feel of the item, will the shoes be comfortable and is the blouse of good quality. Nevertheless, the use of realistic avatars has greatly improved the experience of virtual shopping. Physical items being purchased online are therefore likely to increase. Thus strongly reducing the need for exchange into fiat currency whilst allowing for a good to be integrated into the economy, which if needed can be resold second-hand. The regulatory framework therefore has to include supervision of currencies that have a large redemption rate.

Whilst the above closes the discussion on integration and thereby the traditional three-layered process of MLFT, the Metaverse introduces new risks. The 3-step model to define MLFT is therefore useful as a concept but too limited to encompass all risks associated with the Metaverse. The next paragraphs will discuss three distinct risks associated with the Metaverse reality.

4.3 Additional Risks Associated with the Metaverse

4.3.1 Anonymity

The stages of MLFT are largely the same between virtual MLFT and ordinary MLFT, the introduction of the Metaverse has changed the scope of these risks. The first difference between physical and virtual MLFT risk is that of anonymity. Non-virtual MLFT requires some form of identification or risk of identification. The most obvious is when MLFT is conducted through a bank account, bank accounts within the EU and more broadly are linked to verified persons. Whilst cash is generally anonymous, it can be obtained from or placed into a bank account and thus linking it to a person. Large transactions are reported and even the physical act of obtaining or spending the cash generally includes a person being recorded by security cameras. The need for a person to be present during the spending of the money decreases the anonymity. To decrease the connection between a person and funds, criminals use shell corporations. The corporations create a layer between the owner and the funds. Anonymity within the Metaverse, however, will be achieved more easily.

A user can remain fully anonymous quite easily as there is no legislation requiring the identity verification of users. The danger is that anonymity can spur crime, Kelly and Lynes' research indicates that the anonymity an avatar provides promotes white-collar crime. Their research considered that within virtual reality, users were increasingly willing to commit fraud.[34] This fraud was aimed at taking other users' virtual

---

[34] Kelly and Lynes (2020), p. 114.

assets to gain status. Whilst perhaps not as serious as financing terrorism it indicates the sense of security through anonymity that an avatar provides. When considering virtual currency it is both the avatar and the wallet that needs investigating. This means that when a wallet is not connected to an avatar, the wallet owner needs identification. As demonstrated in the previous sections the Metaverse's interoperability allows for the use of different avatar and payment providers. There is no need for an avatar to be provided by the same company as the payment system. Furthermore, peer-to-peer payments are facilitated on a fairly anonymous basis. This raises the question of whether users should verify the identity of the person they are trading with.

Cassella in his paper considers the situation of a person aiming to finance terrorism. Cassella considers that the person can go through the complicated MLFT stages, or post the money to the right destination.[35] The latter can achieve the same effects as through the earlier defined stages of MLFT. Cassella argues that the person sending the money is worthwhile investigating.[36] Irwin and others consider that MLFT largely occurs through the same channels virtually and physically. However, financing of terrorism prefers methods with high levels of anonymity.[37] It is therefore important to decrease the level of anonymity in the Metaverse. Whereby emphasis should be on those persons who enter the economy which includes the transfer and storage of value. The regulatory framework therefore has to lift the anonymity of the Metaverse economy.

4.3.2 Jurisdiction

In his research, Stokes compares the risks of MLFT via Bitcoin and L$.[38] His research concludes that the risk of illegal activities is enhanced through both Bitcoin and L$. This risk enhancement stems from the anonymity of the platforms, large-scale access and the possibility of peer-to-peer payments without the need for the heavily regulated financial sector.[39] Similar conclusions have been reached with regard to Second Life and WoW by Irwin and Slay.[40] Furthermore, Dyer-Whitford and De Peuter argue that the majority of these parties are located in the Cayman Islands a jurisdiction known for its weak financial regulation.[41] These factors sound numerous but describe two issues.

---

[35] Cassella (2018), p. 495.
[36] Ibid.
[37] Irwin and Choo (2012), pp. 85–111.
[38] Stokes (2012).
[39] Ibid, pp. 225–226.
[40] Irwin and Slay (2010).
[41] Dyer-Witheford and De Peuter (2009), p. xii.

4.3 Additional Risks Associated with the Metaverse

The first is the easy accessibility of parties internationally. The provider of the virtual world and its customers do not require close proximity to transact. The companies providing the virtual world and its payment system can therefore choose to locate in favourable jurisdictions. Favorable in this case means low levels of taxation, legislation or enforcement obligations. These type of jurisdictions are attractive to providers as it saves costs. Additionally, the firms can avoid heavily regulated financial institutions through peer-to-peer payment structures. Peer-to-peer payment without the need for intervention of regulated parties generates high-risk transactions. When making a payment from the EU to a low-regulated jurisdiction through a bank or money transfer agency the transaction is recorded by the financial institution in the EU. This institution should, in case of suspicious transaction levels, report the transactions to the appropriate authority. Peer-to-peer payment systems ensure trust through technologies such as blockchain. Blockchain generates sufficient trust among consumers that their transactions are conducted. These transactions can be conducted without borders whilst avoiding regulated institutions.

The second difficulty with jurisdiction is related to the first. Companies can locate to low regulatory jurisdictions or detach themselves from jurisdictions altogether. The virtual environments in the Metaverse can be created without jurisdiction. A provider of a virtual environment can opt to build the environment without identifying himself. Without an identified provider as a host, it is difficult to determine jurisdiction. The server where the environment is hosted could be traced and used as jurisdiction. This process, however, would be difficult and costly. Therefore those within the environment operate within a vacuum. Providing a financial service in such an environment was difficult as the financial institution required trust from its customers. Very few would trust an unregulated and unbacked financial institution. The peer-to-peer payments however ask that consumers trust the blockchain. The blockchain does not need to be located in a jurisdiction to be considered trustworthy. Thus creating a jurisdictional vacuum.

The regulatory framework therefore has to incorporate a limitation to the type of peer-to-peer transactions. In particular, those that occur without (strongly) regulated payment facilities. Whilst a seemingly impossible task, the alternative is an unregulated space for MLFT. The Metaverse will be compatible with a large amount of virtual reality providers. There is no limitation on where these providers or users are located globally. The Metaverse is therefore likely to be accessible globally thus increasing the risk of regulatory avoidance. A legislative framework therefore has to reduce the potential for avoiding regulations.

These conclude the main aspects of MLFT through the Metaverse. There is, however, another odd occurrence that disserves attention; that of the Non-Fungible Tokens.

4.3.3 Non Fungible Tokens

Non-Fungible Tokens (NFT) are a form of token based upon a blockchain and correspond with a non-fungible item. These items have to be unique such as a painting, collector item or piece of music. The owner of the item can create NFTs based on the item to ensure ownership. The NFT then functions as a form of certificate of originality and ownership in a virtual world.[42] This certificate can be bought and transferred but the (virtual) item does not need to be transferred.[43] The NFTs are considered the virtual equivalent of ownership rights.[44] It is therefore likely that NFTs are a technology to stay for the foreseeable future.[45] Additionally, Metaverse will generate an additional place where digital art can be showcased on virtual walls. Therefore providing an incentive to the digital art market. A market that is already rapidly expanding. The CryptoPunk art with their NFTs has generated a $2.5 billion trade due to their scarcity and uniqueness.[46] The NFTs are traded in a similar fashion as cryptocurrencies. An NFT can be bought through trading platforms or privately and stored in virtual wallets.

NFTs and MLFT are related similarly to physical real estate and artworks. They are objects used as an investment for criminal money. The investment can be used as an object for the personal enjoyment of the criminal. Another use for art is to store value or use art as a payment method.[47] The Financial Action Task Force considers (FATF) that in particular small art objects are used as payment methods or bribes. These objects are easier to move undetected in comparison with bank transfers.[48] The report further identifies that these small objects include digital art stored on USB sticks.[49] In theory therefore these do not particularly include NFTs. Nevertheless, most digital art is worthless without an NFT as it can be easily copied. In addition, many NFTs can be transferred through wallets without moving the physical counterpart. Thereby making it easier to transfer ownership of valuable items without moving the physical item. In addition, the value of NFTs can be artificially increased through "wash trading". Wash trading means that an NFT moves through several wallets of the same owner to appear in high demand and trade ability. It is suspected that this practice has generated an $8.9 million profit in 2021 alone.[50] This facilitates money laundering as art can be cheaply bought and the price inflated through a relatively simple fraud scam. The NFT moves through wallets similar to cryptocurrencies. For the purpose of regulation against MLFT, the NFTs can be

---

[42] Rijmenam (2022), p. 129.
[43] Chohan and Paschen (2021), p. 2.
[44] Ibid.
[45] Press Release Gartner (2021).
[46] Gilmour (2023), p. 681.
[47] FATF (2023), p. 12.
[48] Ibid.
[49] Ibid.
[50] Chainalysis (2022).

4.3 Additional Risks Associated with the Metaverse

regulated and treated as if they are cryptocurrencies. Nevertheless, a new danger of NFT has been discovered. Namely the NFT as a method of transmitting information.

NFTs can contain information software that can be shared between two parties.[51] The transfer of NFTs through these wallets is aimed at sharing information. Providing a safe method of communication as the NFT can be destroyed or burned after receiving the information. The destruction of an NFT is similar to that of a cryptocurrency. An NFT needs to be stored within a virtual wallet. To destroy an NFT it can be sent to a wallet that does not exist. Since the wallet does not exist and can therefore not be accessed the NFT is practically burned. This process cannot be reversed and therefore adds security. When one party is apprehended by a national Financial Intelligence Unit the information on the NFT remains lost. This process of information sharing is therefore attractive to organized crime and terrorist cells.

The risk of information sharing through NFTs should be viewed with some limitations. If a party wishes to finance terrorism, the party needs to ensure the money ends up with the right final party. Under 'ordinary MLFT' any type of funds can reach the other side, meaning it does not need to be exactly the same euro bill or cryptocurrency coin that reaches the other wallet. As described in the paragraphs on layering it is even preferred that not the exact same currency reaches the final destination. As long as a certain value is received at the end of the chain, the initiator is satisfied. When using NFT to transfer information, the exact same NFT that is sent needs to reach the final destination. The NFT process has several groups of stakeholders that are involved in the initial offering of the token.[52] The amount of stakeholders involved in the process of creating and transferring an NFT generates risks.

The first is that a party in between does not transfer the NFT. It may not wish to resell, get confiscated or lost. In this scenario, the information is lost to the sending and receiving parties. Secondly, the in-between party may take some time to resell the NFT, therefore making the information obsolete. Thirdly the information on the NFT could be discovered and decrypted by a third party. Thereby revealing the information to third parties and possibly the authorities. Transmitting information or value through NFTs is therefore risky. The easiest way around these risks is by transferring an NFT directly from the sender to the aimed receiver. Thus generating a direct link between the two parties. This link is encrypted but stored on a public blockchain. A potential investigation can thus more easily trace the entire network.

The risk of information sent through NFTs is not strictly one of financial concern. The aim is to transmit information rather than funding. The criminal intent and potential destructiveness are however no less than crime funding. To discover this process, will require the supervision of wallets as NFTs are held within the same wallet as cryptocurrency. Furthermore, as certificates of ownership NFTs can represent high-value items such as art or real estate. These items are often associated

---

[51] Owen and Chase (2021).
[52] Wilson et al. (2021), p. 8.

with MLFT. This book will therefore include examining NFTs within the legal framework.

4.4 Conclusion

This chapter has examined the risks associated with the Metaverse with regard to MLFT. This risk assessment generated a practical framework to evaluate the current legal approach to MLFT. This chapter has conducted the risk assessment by first analyzing the standard three-step process of MLFT. It then continued by analyzing additional risks that are associated specifically with virtual currencies and the Metaverse. This analysis has generated a set of questions that the legal framework will have to abide by in order to prevent MLFT. These questions were sorted per theme, the first of which is that of placement.

The potential routes via which to place funds into the Metaverse are diverse. Whilst diversity is not per se an issue, it provides a difficulty for the legislative framework. The legislative framework has to encompass all methods of placing funds into the Metaverse under supervision. It is furthermore likely that technology will continue to develop. Therefore the legislative framework either has to continue changing, or not be limited to technologies currently in existence. Furthermore, to place funds into the financial system, smurfing is a popular method. This method is facilitated by the Metaverse environment through the integration of smart contracts and the ease of owning multiple wallets. The second phase of MLFT is the layering of funds to disable the tracing of the (criminal) origin. Due to the speed of blockchain transactions and the lack of clearing institutions, layering is fairly easy. The transactions occur in real time thus limiting transaction monitoring.[53] In particular transactions through the Metaverse can be done rather quickly worldwide. A high risk is the potential use of disguising mechanisms such as mixing services and TOR networks. The integration phase is the phase whereby the funds are integrated into the legal economy. The legal economy in the Metaverse is, however, different from the normal concept of legal economy. The consumption of virtual items can be equated to real consumption. The legislative framework should therefore be considerate of the change in the real economy. In addition to the traditional phases of MLFT, this chapter discovered risks specific to the Metaverse. These have been identified as anonymity, accessibility and NFTs. To effectively regulate the Metaverse a legal framework should incorporate these new risks.

The establishment of these risks specific to the Metaverse says little about the current legal framework. The next chapters will examine the legal approach adopted by the EU and evaluate whether it effectively addresses these issues. The chapters are structured along the different MLFT phases and evaluate the legal framework and where needed introduce suggestions for improvement.

---

[53] Campbell-Verduyn (2018), p. 287.

References

Albrecht C, Duffin K (2019) The use of cryptocurrencies in the money laundering process. J Money Laundering Control 22(2):210–216

Bray D, Konsynski B (2006) Virtual worlds, virtual economies, virtual institutions. Virtual Worlds and New Realities Conference at Emory University 2008

Campbell-Verduyn M (2018) Bitcoin, crypto-coins, and global anti-money laundering governance. Crime Law Soc Chang 69:283–305

Cassella SD (2018) Toward a new model of money laundering. Is the "placement, layering, integration model obsolete?". J Money Laund Control 21

Chainalysis (2022) Crime and NFTs: chainalysis detects significant wash trading and some NFT money laundering in this emerging asset class, available at: https://blog.chainalysis.com/reports/2022-crypto-crime-report-preview-nft-wash-trading-money-laundering. Accessed 07 Aug 2023

Chohan R, Paschen J (2021) What marketers need to know about non-fungible tokens (NFTs). Bus Horiz. (in press)

Cuthbertson A (13 January 2019) How children playing Fortnite are helping to fuel organised crime. The Independent

Dong Y, Kourtellis N, Hammer B, Lozano J (eds) (2021) Machine learning and knowledge discovery in databases. Springer, Cham

Dostov V, Shust P (2014) Customer loyalty programs: money laundering and terrorism financing risks. J Money Laund Control 17(4):385–394

Dupuis D, Gleason K (2022) Money laundering in a CBDC world: a game of cats and mice. J Financ Crime 29(1)

Dyer-Witheford N, De Peuter G (2009) Games of empire. Global capitalism and video games. University of Minnesota Press, Minneapolis

Dyntu V, Dykyi O (2018) Cryptocurrency in the system of money laundering. Baltic J Econ Stud 4(5):75. https://doi.org/10.30525/2256-0742/2018-4-5-75-81

FATF (2023) Money laundering and terrorist financing in the art and antiquities market. Paris

Gilmour P (2023) Non-fungible tokens: CryptoPunks and the art of wash trading. J Money Laund Control

Irwin A, Choo K (2012) An analysis of money laundering and terrorism financing typologies. J Money Laund Control 15(1):85–111

Irwin A, Slay J (2010) Detecting money laundering and terrorism financing activity in second life and World of Warcraft. International Cyber Resilience Conference

Keene S (2012) Emerging threats: financial crime in the virtual world. J Money Laund Control 15(1)

Kelly C, Lynes A (2020) The democratization of white-collar criminality in video games. In: Kelly C, Lynes A (eds) Video games crime and next-gen deviance. Emerald (online)

Mabunda S (2018) Cryptocurrency: the new face of cyber money laundering. IEEE, p 4

Mbiyavanga S (2019) Cryptolaundering: anti-money laundering regulation of virtual currency. Exchanges J Anti-Corrup Law 3(1)

Metaverse (2022) Homepage. https://mvs.org/

Mooij A (2022a) Toezicht op virtuele valuta: de wereld van het gamen. SEW Tijdschrift voor Europees en economisch recht 3

Mooij A (2022b) A digital euro for everyone: can the European system of central banks introduce general purpose CBDC as part of its economic mandate? J Bank Regul 24:89–10

Nagy H, Mezei K (2016) The organised criminal phenomenon on the internet. Eastern-Eur Criminal Law 2

Owen A, Chase I (2021) NFTs: a new frontier for money. https://rusi.org/explore-our-research/publications/commentary/nfts-new-frontier-money-laundering

Press Release Gartner (23 August 2021) Gartner identifies key emerging technologies spurring innovation through trust, growth and change, Available on https://www.gartner.com/en/

newsroom/press-releases/2021-08-23-gartner-identifies-key-emerging-technologies-spurring-innovation-through-trust-growth-and-change

Renteria N, Wilson T, Strohecker K (2021) In a world first, El Salvador makes bitcoin legal tender, Reuters 10 June

Richet J (2013) Laundering money online: a review of cybercriminals' methods', Tools and Resources for Anti-Corruption Knowledge – June, 01, 2013 – United Nations Office on Drugs and Crime (UNODC)

Rijmenam M (2022) Step into the Metaverse. How the immersive internet will unlock a trillion-dollar social economy. Wiley, Hoboken

Stokes R (2012) Virtual money laundering: the case of bitcoin and the Linden dollar. Inf Commun Technol 21

Terdiman D (2007) 'eBay bans auction of virtual goods. Sale of items from Warcraft and Everquest are now a no-no, but eBay gives the OK for items from Second Life', CNet 30 january https://www.cnet.com/news/ebay-bans-auctions-of-virtual-goods/

Van den Broek M (2015) Preventing money laundering: a legal study on the effectiveness of supervision in the European Union. Eleven International Publishing, The Hague

Vandezande N (2017) Virtual currencies under EU anti-money laundering law. Comp Law Security Rev 33(3):341–353

Weeks-Brown R (2018) Countries are advancing efforts to stop criminals from laundering their trillions. IMF Finance & Development Magazine

Wilson K, Karg A, Ghaderi H (2021) Prospecting non-fungible tokens in the digital economy: stakeholders and ecosystem, risk and opportunity. Business Horizons (in press)

Open Access This chapter is licensed under the terms of the Creative Commons Attribution 4.0 International License (http://creativecommons.org/licenses/by/4.0/), which permits use, sharing, adaptation, distribution and reproduction in any medium or format, as long as you give appropriate credit to the original author(s) and the source, provide a link to the Creative Commons license and indicate if changes were made.

The images or other third party material in this chapter are included in the chapter's Creative Commons license, unless indicated otherwise in a credit line to the material. If material is not included in the chapter's Creative Commons license and your intended use is not permitted by statutory regulation or exceeds the permitted use, you will need to obtain permission directly from the copyright holder.

Chapter 5
Regulating the Technology (Placement)

5.1 Introduction: The EU Approach to the Placement of Funds

This chapter will discuss the legal framework in place and the framework needed to regulate the Metaverse to reduce MLFT at the placement phase. Whilst the primary focus of this chapter will be the placement phase some of the proposals will have a spill-over into the other stages of MLFT. The legal framework will be limited to that of the European Union. The EU's AMLD was updated in 2018 through the introduction of AMLD5 with the aim to include supervision of virtual currencies.[1] Specifically, the AMLD5 includes the supervision of fiat/crypto exchange services and virtual wallets.

The EU therefore theoretically has covered the supervision of the placement phase. To insert cryptocurrency requires an exchange from fiat currency to a virtual wallet. Furthermore, any cryptocurrency paid in return for criminal activities is also supervised through the supervision of wallets. The system furthermore mimics the supervision of banks in the sense that similar monitoring duties are assigned. Nevertheless, there are some differences. The first is the general approach that the providers of exchange and storage services have to register not apply for a license. Additionally, the registration within one EU country does not generate authority to provide these services in other EU countries. Prima facie the EU therefore has opted for a system with little cooperation between the Member States. Initially a bad sign for approaching such a global issue. Furthermore the registration seems a softer requirement than that of the licensing used for other financial institutes.

The approach, however, does not necessarily have to reduce the effectiveness of the legal framework. That a registration is not valid throughout the EU is perhaps bad

---

[1] Directive (EU) 2018/843 of the European Parliament and of the Council of 30 May 2018 amending Directive (EU) 2015/849 on the prevention of the use of the financial system for the purposes of money laundering or terrorist financing, and amending Directives 2009/138/EC and 2013/36/EU.

© The Author(s) 2024
A. Mooij, *Regulating the Metaverse Economy*, SpringerBriefs in Law, https://doi.org/10.1007/978-3-031-46417-1_5

for the internal market and it may also increase the burden for the institutions offering these services. This, however, does not have to reduce the effectiveness of the supervisory system. More importantly, the question is whether all possibilities of entering funds into the Metaverse have been incorporated into the legal framework.

5.2 Entity

To encompass all methods of placing funds into the Metaverse the definition of a wallet has to incorporate all forms of wallets. The AMLD5 defines a wallet provider as:

> "custodian wallet provider" means an entity that provides services to safeguard private cryptographic keys on behalf of its customers, to hold, store and transfer virtual currencies.[2]

With this definition, the custodian wallets are brought under the supervision of national entities. Wallet providers will have to register with national supervisors and conduct the duties specific to the jurisdiction. In the Netherlands these duties flow forth from the Wet ter voorkoming van witwassen en financiering van terrorisme (Wwft)[3] and the Sanctiewet.[4] These duties include the verification of the identity of customers and reporting of suspicious transactions. Prima facie the directive in combination with national supervision would seriously hamper any anonymous transactions taking place in the Metaverse. This would theoretically mitigate a large risk factor of MLFT, as the wallet is generally considered to provide anonymity.[5] To do so, however, it needs to cover all forms of wallets that can be found in the Metaverse.

As stated in the second chapter there are three primary routes through which funds can be held in the Metaverse. Those are separate wallet providers, through the avatar and through the reality provider. The regulation is broadly formulated using the word 'entity'. The term entity is by no means a clear definition. Godlieb considers that the Commission is particularly vague on this topic.[6] Unclear legislation is generally undesirable, in this case, however, it should be considered positive. Technology is an ever-changing organism and therefore legal statutes are often obsolete before they are published. The European Banking Authority considered there were more than 200 different types of virtual currency in existence in 2014, the report further expected more would be developing every day.[7] In 2022 there were

---

[2] Ibid, article 1.
[3] Law in order to prevent money laundering and the financing of terrorism.
[4] Sanction law.
[5] Del Monaco (2020), p. 6.
[6] Godlieb (2018).
[7] European Banking Authority (2014), p. 10.

5.2 Entity

over 18,000 different cryptocurrencies available.[8] Technology continues to develop and detailed legislation would only play catch-up. Open terminology in law based upon intention can halt the technology race that currently exists between lawmakers and criminals.[9] Fairfield argues that good law should have a sense of stability and innovation.[10] The language of law should thus encompass new technologies.[11] The most straightforward approach is to use open language without (unnecessary) details. Open language with fewer details risks a conflict with legal certainty. Legal certainty is a concept that requires the law to be sufficiently clear so its subjects know their rights and duties. Open language does not necessarily provide the clarity needed to know one's duties. Nevertheless, open language does not have to conflict with legal certainty if its practices are sufficiently clear.

The law on paper and the law in practice should be considered independently. Laws that seem vague can have a legal practice surrounding them that is far clearer.[12] Legal statutes can therefore be phrased rather openly if the intention of the law is clear. Consider the smuggling of drugs. The legislation includes the (intention) to pass a border with illegal substances. How the substance passes the border, whether the substance is hidden on the person's body or within their suitcase is irrelevant. The practice surrounding the law makes it clear that it includes all forms of drug smuggling. The question is whether the same can be said from the MLFT framework. Is the intention of MLFT regulated whilst the term entity includes all forms of technology?

The intention of the legal framework is quite clear, namely to prevent MLFT. As discussed in the previous chapter, money laundering is a process of moving money from the illegal economy to the legal economy. The final stage includes the conversion of money into assets of value. To regulate the intention of money laundering therefore requires the regulation of moving value from the illegal to the legal economy. Similarly, financing of terrorism has the intention of moving value to a terrorist group. This broad definition does not have to form a legal obstacle. The EU regulation implementing sanctions against specific terrorist groups is equally broad. It considers providing any economic advantage or economic resources. The latter is defined as any form of tangible or intangible asset or fund.[13] The term money laundering within the AMLD is equally broadly defined for criminal law purposes. The intention is therefore regulated broadly for criminal law purposes but then

---

[8] Howarth (2022).

[9] Kelly and Lynes (2020), p. 295.

[10] Fairfield (2021), p. 70.

[11] Ibid.

[12] Brownsword and Somsen (2009), p. 68.

[13] Article 1(1)(2) Council Regulation (EC) No 881/2002 of 27 May 2002 imposing certain specific restrictive measures directed against certain persons and entities associated with Usama bin Laden, the Al-Qaida network and the Taliban, and repealing Council Regulation (EC) No 467/2001 prohibiting the export of certain goods and services to Afghanistan, strengthening the flight ban and extending the freeze of funds and other financial resources in respect of the Taliban of Afghanistan.

changes direction. The AMLD does not consider all entities offering services that can be used for money laundering, but rather it creates a list of services that fall within the scope of the AMLD5. For legal certainty purposes, it makes sense to create a list. Lists are clear, however by generating the list the AMLD has excluded risky technologies. In particular with regard to the exclusion of non-custodian wallets.

Preamble 8 of AMLD5 defines the aim of bringing the custodian wallet providers within the legal framework. It considers that by placing these wallets under supervision terrorists will find it more difficult to transfer funds into the EU.[14] The term entity in combination with this aim should therefore be considered as any custodian entity that enables funds to be transferred from and to its domain of supervision. Whether this entity also provides other services, such as providing an avatar or virtual location, should not matter. It therefore is an appropriate use of a vague term entity. Whilst the definition of entities is broadly formulated there is an important restriction to the type of wallets that are regulated. To avoid the anonymity of transfers the AMLD5 included custodian wallet providers within the scope of the directive.[15] The AMLD5, however, states that this inclusion will not fully break through the anonymity because transactions can occur without custodian wallet providers.[16] Leaving out the non-custodian wallets forms a risk to the integrity of the Metaverse environment.

5.3 Custodian and Non-custodian Wallets

The impact assessment from the European Commission considers that the framework should cover all custodian wallets.[17] Leaving out players would drastically reduce the effect of the AMLD5.[18] The Dutch legislator further adds that financial institutions have a gateway function to the economy.[19] To purposefully exclude wallets would therefore be contrary to the intention of the AMLD5. Nevertheless, the wallets have been separated into two categories. The "custodian" and "non-custodian" wallets. The AMLD5 only places the custodian wallet under its legal framework.[20] The difference between the two depends on the safekeeping of the

---

[14] Cassella (2018).

[15] Ibid, recital 8.

[16] Ibid, recital 9.

[17] COMMISSION STAFF WORKING DOCUMENT IMPACT ASSESSMENT Accompanying the document Proposal for a Directive of the European Parliament and the Council amending Directive (EU) 2015/849 on the prevention of the use of the financial system for the purposes of money laundering or terrorist financing and amending Directive 2009/101/EC.

[18] Ibid, Sect. 8.2.

[19] *Kamerstukken II* 2018/19, 35245, 3, p. 3.

[20] AMDL5, article 1(19).

5.3 Custodian and Non-custodian Wallets

encryption key. The transfer of cryptocurrencies requires two keys. A public key acts like an address and a private key is the proof-of-ownership code. The keys are somewhat comparable to the numbers involved in a bank account. The public key is the bank account number, to which the money is transferred. The private key on the other hand is like the PIN that is needed to transfer the money. The custodian wallet acts like a bank vault that stores both money and PIN. If you lose access to your vault (custodian wallet) the bank can grant you access after verifying your identity.

A non-custodian wallet, however, does not safeguard the encryption key. The owner of the cryptocurrency has to remember the private key to transfer the cryptocurrency. If the user loses the key, the currency cannot be traded anymore. The currency will be stuck within the account, like a vault with only one key once the key is lost so are its contents. There are two types of non-custodian wallets. The first is the so-called hot wallets, which are permanently connected to the internet. The second category is the cold wallets, which can be disconnected and stored offline. These would include wallets such as hardware (stored on USB) or even good old-fashioned paper wallets. To move currency to another wallet, all wallets need an internet connection. As it is the wallet does not actually store the currency as a physical wallet. The wallet is the gateway to interacting with the blockchain.[21] This gateway can only interact with the blockchain through connection. A piece of paper can store the keys but to transact the user will need to install a software wallet. Similarly, a USB can be kept offline whilst storing your currency but to transact it will need to use the internet.

Concerning the Metaverse this division means that any wallet that is provided as a service, the custodian wallet, would be part of the supervisory framework. An avatar or virtual room provider that provides a password-protected payment service to its customer would have to comply with the AMLD5. The wallets that are offered without storing private keys would not. This division is based on the notion that a software provider cannot monitor the client's transactions.[22] The software provider sells the wallet and is then considered disconnected from the wallet. Whilst a restaurant can check whether the customer eats his or her vegetables, the grocery store that sells vegetables cannot verify that the customer eats the produce. The result is that the non-custodian wallets have not been given any duties with regard to MLFT. The non-custodian wallets in particular the hardware wallets, are however considered much safer. Storing a piece of paper or USB stick carries the risk of damage or loss but hacking a USB or piece of paper not connected to the internet is impossible.

There are two different views with regard to the regulation of non-custodian wallets. The first vision is that non-custodian wallets should not be regulated. The argument is that cash is also unregulated and anonymous.[23] This argument, however, is largely incorrect. Firstly because large cash transactions are generally considered

---

[21] Azman and Sharma (2020), pp. 306–307.
[22] *Kamerstukken II* 2018/19, 35245, 3, p. 4.
[23] Haffke et al. (2019), p. 135.

suspicious and reported. Secondly, cash in the eurozone often is acquired through a regulated bank. Few people receive their wages, benefits or other form of income in cash. Therefore large sums of cash are either acquired through a bank withdrawal. When spending large sums of cash it is considered suspicious and customer verification duties apply. Furthermore, a cash transfer, unless sent by post, requires physical nearness and is slow. Unlike the transfer through virtual currency which is fast and does not require the sender and receiver to be in physical proximity. It is therefore not a convincing argument to say that cash is unregulated and therefore there is no need to regulate non-custodian wallets. The second vision regarding not regulating non-custodian wallets is that they cannot perform monitoring duties. This vision is considered more often and is more serious, than the cash argument but is not perse correct either. In particular when examining the extent of the duties the wallets have to perform in order to be registered as a wallet provider.

Wallet services have to register with the national supervisory authority in order to provide their services. The extent of the duties in order to complete this registration was under discussion in a lower court case in the Netherlands.[24] In this case, the wallet provider was asked by the Dutch Central Bank (DNB) to complete customer verification per transaction. The judge in the case considered that such requirements by the DNB were unlikely to be in compliance with the EU legislation. As the judge considered the EU legislator had opted for a registration system rather than a licensing system.[25] In particular, the judge considered the wallet provider had taken other measures to prevent MLFT. These measures included customer verification when the account was set up. The company furthermore only accepted customers with Single Euro Payments Area (SEPA) regulated bank accounts.[26] The judge therefore considered that it would be unlikely that the customer verification required by DNB would be in compliance with EU law.[27] The judge in question did not give a final ruling as to this matter, only suspicions. The merits of the case were not discussed in depth as it concerned a preliminary provision hearing. Nevertheless, the judge divided the duties into two categories. The first set of duties are the due diligence measures taken by the wallet provider to comply with the Know Your Customer (KYC) principles at the moment of registration. The second set of duties was the due diligence that is exercised when transferring into the real economy. In this case by only allowing customers to convert virtual currency into fiat currency to their own (supervised) SEPA account. The DNB's measures were aimed at per-transaction due diligence. The per-transaction verification is focused on a continuing monitoring process. The latter was rejected by the Dutch lower court as a duty. To argue therefore that the exclusion of non-custodian wallets is based on

---

[24] Rechtbank Rotterdam 07 april 2021, ECLI:NL:RBROT:2021:2968.

[25] Ibid, r.o. 6.5.

[26] Ibid.

[27] Ibid. The suspicion of the judge was not a definitive judgement as it concerned a preliminary relief procedure. There was no substantive procedure as the requirements were lifted by DNB shortly after the preliminary relief judgement.

monitoring seems redundant. Rather the question should be asked whether the software provider can conduct due diligence when selling the software. And secondly, whether transactions can be monitored when these are transferred from or into fiat currency.

Customer verification entails that the provider of the wallet knows the customer's identity. There are two options with regard to customer identification upon sale. The first is a physical in-store verification. In this case, the customer would have to purchase the software in a physical store and present identification upon purchase. This process could be introduced quite easily. There is, however, a risk if this is the only approach used. The more regulation that is applicable to providers, the more difficult it is for start-ups to enter the market. It may even overburden small enterprises and push them out of the market.[28] If all software providers have to offer a physical shop where they sell the software and customers are mandated to make their purchase in a physical location, this may hinder competition. The burden of such regulation is therefore a good argument to limit regulation, perhaps even abolish customer due diligence. Regulation, however, aims to protect and create a fair and safe market. Preventing the financing of crime and terrorism is an obvious example of a goal that regulation should aim to achieve. A balance must be found between protecting the public good and allowing new or smaller actors to enter and remain in the market. In order to achieve such a balance the financial services provisions market should be analyzed.

Two observations can be made with regard to the market structure. The first is that the products provided can be considered a service (in the case of custodian wallets) and a software app (in the case of non-custodian wallets). The production of apps is generally considered a competitive market. This is particularly true because the competition in app stores is fierce.[29] The main risk of regulating highly competitive markets is inappropriate and unevenly enforced regulation.[30] The regulation should therefore be limited to what is needed and be equal within the EU. However, there is a second observation namely the risk associated with inflexible regulation.[31] Providing payment infrastructure originally depended upon the institution having a banking permit. The permits resulted in high barriers to entry[32] and there was very limited competition. The requirement of physical due diligence would raise high barriers for wallet providers, as shops would be needed at various locations. Competition between banks is good for the consumers,[33] it is difficult for consumers to switch to a different bank thus decreasing competition in the banking sector.[34] Switching from wallet to wallet, however, is more flexible. The relative monopoly

---

[28] Keene (2012).
[29] Pierce and Wooldridge (2014), p. 2.
[30] Beardsley and Farrell (2005), p. 52.
[31] Ibid, p. 53.
[32] The high barriers in particularly were the capital requirements placed upon banks.
[33] Bikker and Bos (2005), pp. 103–104.
[34] WRR (2019), pp. 137–138.

that banks had on providing payment services through the permit system is changing. The wallet market may increase competition but it needs dynamic and flexible regulation.[35] Thus providing ample reason to abandon the need for due diligence, as these are the most burdensome for service providers.[36] However, the size and speed of MLFT are changing too and as discussed earlier the virtual currencies increase the risk of MLFT. It therefore does not seem prudent to abolish with due diligence. Rather the question is whether due diligence can be done more cost-efficiently through remote verification.

The identity of an individual wishing to purchase an application can be remotely uploaded and verified. Banks have been operating through online verification to open a payment account for several years. Biometrical information can be dependently verified through mobile devices under various circumstances.[37] A copy of a passport combined with facial recognition could ensure the software provider has knowledge of the identity of their customer. This process will be further facilitated with the introduction of the European Digital Identity. A project currently conducted by the European Commission in order to facilitate digital identity verification for citizens.[38] Linking this verification process to the database of persons who have sanctions enforced upon them would provide effective due diligence. Currently, similar proposals are being considered by the European Central Bank. Their report on the digital euro includes a discussion of a bearer (or token-based) digital euro. In their analysis of how the bearer digital euro would be designed, the ECB considers the device capable of identifying the user's identity.[39] A device (such as a mobile phone) and application able to identify the user should not be considered futuristic. Rather it can be used and should be incorporated within regulation. Slightly more difficult is to verify a corporate client. The wallet has to establish a corporate management structure. Whilst this process is somewhat more difficult, this identification can be done through official documents of the Chamber of Commerce (CoC) or notarized documents. Furthermore, since 2020 Member States have begun implementing the Ultimate Beneficial Ownership (UBO) register. This register was due to be completed on the 27th of March 2022. This register can be used as an aid to verify ownership structures. Some company structures have been excluded from the duty to register. Hence it is likely the verification would be done through a combination of the CoC, notarized and UBO documents. Thus demonstrating that remote due diligence is not impossible and does not need human interaction. Remote due diligence is more affordable for software developers and could break the

---

[35] Kelly and Lynes (2020), p. 55.

[36] Rajput (2013), p. 3.

[37] Wójtowicz and Joachimiak (2016), pp. 195–207.

[38] European Commission. Digital Identity for all Europeans (last accessed 10 May 2022) available at: https://ec.europa.eu/info/strategy/priorities-2019-2024/europe-fit-digital-age/european-digital-identity_en.

[39] European Central Bank (2020), p. 30.

anonymity of non-custodial wallets. The non-custodian wallets could therefore abide by the first set of rules identified by the Dutch court.

The second set of duties the judge court identified is when virtual currency is converted into fiat currency. The company in the Dutch case was considered to abide by that obligation because they only accepted transactions to and from SEPA accounts. These SEPA accounts had to be registered with the owner. Non-custodian wallets could have a similar limitation, whereby the software can only conduct transactions with the owner's own SEPA account. Theoretically, this would fulfil all the duties set by the Dutch judge. Unfortunately, it is not that simple when considering the Metaverse implications. The wallet in the Dutch case was exclusively used to buy and sell cryptocurrency. The function of the cryptocurrency was comparable to that of an investment portfolio. The wallets used in the Metaverse will however be focused on being used as payment facilitation. Thus requiring the possibility to transact with third parties. The possibility to transact with third parties entails the need to monitor transactions. Transaction monitoring is a continuous process that needs to be conducted by either an external party (such as the original developer) or the wallet itself. The first option is not very different from custodian wallets. The second option is therefore more interesting but requires a new way of thinking; namely through the concept of digital entities.

5.4 Digital Entity

The monitoring process is divided into four stages; risk identification, risk analysis, risk management and risk monitoring.[40] There have been various risks pre-identified by the FATF.[41] The risks can be categorized into two different sets of criteria. The first are the objective risks. In the case of wallets, this includes transactions with a value of €15,000.[42] Furthermore, wallets have to report transactions when they suspect these transactions involve a form of MLFT. These suspicions are based on subjective criteria. Subjective criteria are mostly identifiable through various reports. An example of this is transactions to countries with high MLFT risks, such as those identified by the Commission.[43] However subjective criteria also include other non-identified criteria. These would include a shop whereby a lot of transactions are conducted in cash. Or a shop where the takings are considerably different from its competitors. The detection of these suspicious transactions based on subjective risk

---

[40] De Nederlandsche Bank (2020), p. 15.

[41] European Banking Authority Joint Guidelines under Articles 17 and 18(4) of Directive (EU) 2015/849 on simplified and enhanced customer due diligence and the factors credit and financial institutions should consider when assessing the money laundering and terrorist financing risk associated with individual business relationships and occasional transactions.

[42] Uitvoeringsbesluit Wwft 2018.

[43] EU policy on high-risk third countries. Based on Directive (EU)2015/849.

criteria is no longer a manual process but one conducted through algorithms.[44] The algorithm can contain the coding needed in order to identify such risks. The hits generated by the algorithm are manually inspected and reported to the FIU. The question is whether this human intervention is needed. The algorithm could be directly linked to the FIU and report when suspicious activities occur. This process would eliminate the need for a software developer to remain involved. It may sound ridiculous to take out the human activity. However, in the detection of MLFT, many of the processes have been replaced by technology. Manual activity within the detection of suspicious transactions is already limited.[45] To successfully set up a system whereby AI replaces human intervention, requires two criteria to be met.

The first criterion is that for an algorithm to bring forth the appropriate amount of results, neither too few nor too many, the algorithm needs to work. Whilst algorithms do aid in the detection of MLFT, there are different interpretations about what algorithms are (most) efficient. Some argue in favour of an algorithm based on finding outliers.[46] Whereby the algorithm finds the transactions that are considered unconventional based on conventional payments. The opposite, however, is also argued. Whereby the algorithm aims to detect MLFT based on patterns of MLFT.[47] To decide what is the most efficient algorithm is not a straightforward choice. For such a system to work a choice, however, must be made on what is an acceptable level of efficiency. This choice is furthermore made difficult because the algorithm must also be able to detect suspicious activity for NFTs. NFTs are a relatively new technology, in comparison with cryptocurrencies. However, the large amount of fraudulent activity through NFTs has attracted the attention of various scholars. These scholars have proposed various strategies to detect wash trading with NFTs through algorithms.[48] Some argue a visual confirmation of the data will always be necessary.[49] This however is not a particular problem as the algorithm is used to flag a potential illegal situation. The confirmation can be ensured by the FIU. The second criterion for successfully linking an algorithm to the FIU is that of reducing false positives.

It is the task of the responsible financial institution to sieve through the results of the algorithm and decide which transactions to report. If the results of the algorithm were directly linked to the FIU this would increase the investigative task of the FIU. With custodian wallets, the commercial supervisor investigates the hits and filters through to spot false positives. This job aims to limit the amount of false positives with the FIU. Based upon data from 2019 the FIU in the Netherlands received 68.000 notifications of suspicious transactions, the FIU considered 15.000 of these

---

[44] Van Eerten and Van Heugten (2018), p. 137.
[45] Ibid.
[46] Gao (2009); Kannan and Somasundaram (2017), pp. 190–202.
[47] Soltani et al. (2016).
[48] Serneels (2023) and Von Wachter et al. (2022).
[49] Wen et al. (2023).

5.4 Digital Entity

notifications to be suspicious.[50] That means that the accuracy of these notifications is a little above 22%. An algorithm that has a false positive ratio of 22% or less is therefore an acceptable rate to give direct notice to the FIU. The accuracy and efficiency of recent algorithms have severely improved. A recently developed algorithm claims a 90% accuracy in detecting ML groups. It further claims a 96% accuracy in discovering ML accounts.[51] Higher levels of accuracy can be obtained but with the tradeoff of a higher number of false positives. The monitoring could then effectively be done by the wallet itself if it can achieve high detection levels without more than 22% false positives. Whilst it is therefore technically possible to link an algorithm to the FIU, the question raises who is responsible in case of possible mistakes.

You cannot make an omelette without breaking eggs. Similarly, you cannot run an algorithm without encountering biases. Using an algorithm to monitor suspicious transactions entails the potential for biases and thus claims for damages. The question is who is responsible and liable for the damages? The algorithm? The following paragraphs argue that it is possible to consider algorithms as digital entities. And hold the digital entity responsible for the potential damages.

The term 'entity' which was mentioned before, is broadly formulated. It would likely include any service provider that facilitates wallets whether this is the provider's main focus or not. However, when disconnecting the monitoring process from the software provider to the algorithm, the algorithm has to comply with the law. If the algorithm complies with the legal requirements, it can be connected to the FIU. If the algorithm does not comply with the legal requirements, it cannot be connected to the FIU and should be considered inappropriate for use on the EU market. The term 'entity' is broad but not particularly aimed at a piece of software primarily based upon an algorithm. To think about algorithms or codes as subject to law or part of the legal framework, however, is not new. The software can determine what actions are or are not allowed in a certain setting.[52] Though regulators increasingly rely on codes to execute law there are some difficulties with this approach.

The first obstacle is the rigidity of regulation.[53] The rules in code are inflexible and stringent, rather than decisions made on a case-by-case basis. The flip side is that algorithms can detect suspicious transactions before they occur and can prevent them from happening or at the very least warn their users.[54] Theoretically, a transaction could be prevented from occurring if too suspicious. Such an approach would solve the problem of the finality of transactions. The problem whereby transactions conducted over a blockchain are difficult or near impossible to reverse. However, it would also make it difficult to conduct legitimate transactions deemed as

---

[50] Nederlandse Vereniging van Banken (2019).
[51] Soltani et al. (2016), p. 6.
[52] Hassan and De Filippi (2017), p. 89.
[53] Ibid.
[54] Ibid.

Fig. 5.1 Simple algorithm

suspicious. Theoretically, such actions could be prohibited unless prior permission is given by a certified institution (i.e. notary), yet these would be costly and time-consuming. The second issue with reliance upon algorithms is that they can be discriminatory.[55]

The algorithm is programmed by humans and can have human flaws written into it. Furthermore, this bias can be perpetuated and reinforced by the algorithm.[56] Depending on the consequences, these biases can have a large impact on the users.[57] It should be noted that the problem of bias occurs with human supervision as well. However, in such a case the (legal)person is liable for the damages. The supervising entities using the algorithm are then responsible for being able to explain the decision, thus preventing a black box.[58] The liability in case of biases or other reasons for damages with an independent algorithm is not necessarily clear. Some argue the developer is responsible for any damage that occurs, therefore the software itself would not need a liability framework.[59] However, others argue that a legal framework not adapted to the use of algorithm-based software as legal subjects, risks the formation of accountability gaps.[60] The risks of accountability gaps with regard to non-custodian wallets are highly likely.

In the case of non-custodian wallets in particular it raises questions such as who (or what) is responsible for biases? Or who is responsible for ensuring a consistent level of efficiency over time? These questions are difficult to answer. The algorithm used for the wallets can take two shapes. The first is a normal code that does not adjust and the second is a self-learning algorithm. The simple algorithm is what is used most often. It includes coding and data placed into the algorithm by the user, see Fig. 5.1.

In case of damages, the easy solution is to hold the user responsible for the algorithm. Generally speaking, this is based upon the concept of a "right to an

---

[55] Köchling and Wehner (2020), pp. 795–848.
[56] Baer (2019).
[57] In the Netherlands a bias in the enforcement system of the Dutch tax collection led to the wrongful conviction of people as fraudulent.
[58] De Nederlandsche Bank. Visie op toezicht 2021–2024 available at: https://www.dnb.nl/media/43cnkobx/visie_op_toezicht_2021_2024.pdf.
[59] Ziemianin (2021), pp. 1–22.
[60] Schirmer (2020), p. 128.

5.4 Digital Entity

Fig. 5.2 Non-custodian wallet algorithm

explanation" whereby the developer or user has to be able to explain how the algorithm generates a decision.[61] This specific explanation is commonly entailed in national jurisdictions. The right to an explanation in France is codified through the right of subjective explanation in its Digital Republic Act.[62] In the Netherlands, a similar right has been formulated by the Council of State to emphasize party equality.[63] The responsibility for explanation would thus be on the FIU. Whilst technically possible this would increase the burden on the FIU. Furthermore, a simple algorithm would have difficulty maintaining a high level of accuracy over time. The amount of updating would thus force a more active role on the developer. Thereby creating a hybrid form of wallet, whereby the transactions are not monitored but the algorithm is. This duty might be difficult for small developers. The more effective alternative is that of a complex algorithm that is connected to (risk) databases and is self-learning. In particular, the algorithm is also provided with feedback from (non)successful cases of MLFT and updates on subjective risk catalogues. The algorithm then relies on its coding, which comes from the developer, variously identified criteria and feedback from the supervisor (see Fig. 5.2).

The self-learning algorithm is the most efficient as risk factors can be automatically updated and increase its efficiency through a feedback loop. Whereby the algorithm is provided with feedback on which cases were involved with MLFT. This makes the algorithm more efficient but also creates legal complexity. For example, the algorithm mentioned earlier that claims a 90–96% accuracy rate, is based on clustering technology.[64] The clustering technology is one whereby the algorithm learns unsupervised. Unsupervised learning means that the algorithm can learn from unlabeled data sets. Thereby reducing the need for human intervention. Whilst this technology increases the algorithm's efficiency and reduces intervention it creates a conundrum. The reduction of human intervention makes it difficult for the human to understand why the algorithm has reached an outcome. In particular, a developer will have little influence over or knowledge of the feedback the algorithm receives from the FIU. Thus it is difficult to hold the developer or user accountable for a

---

[61] Edwards and Veale (2018), pp. 46–54.
[62] Ibid, p. 48.
[63] Raad van State 17 mei 2017, ECLI:NL:RVS:2017:1259.
[64] Soltani et al. (2016).

decision made without the explicit understanding and consent of the developer.[65] Other suggested solutions such as reprogramming in case of malfunctioning the algorithm may not be efficient either. Without understanding why the algorithm fails it is difficult to predict whether reprogramming is the solution.[66] Additionally when considering that in case of bias, the solution is reprogramming, one effectively creates a legal responsibility upon the algorithm. The algorithm either must be reprogrammed or be rendered non-compliant with the legal framework. The notion of holding the algorithm responsible would be a solution to the debate on accountability. A piece of software, however, cannot simply be classified as a biological being or a company.[67] The EU Parliament therefore recommended that AI should be given a new classification specific to its digital identity.[68]

Such a new classification, however, raises various questions about the legal framework.[69] To distill the legal framework it is necessary to distinguish between two different sets of AI. The first is one whereby the algorithm is a tool used by humans to extend their abilities. Such a classification generates less legal complexities as it is the human who is using the tool and thus is responsible. The second classification is when AI replaces human performance. This type of AI requires a more comprehensive set of rights and duties.[70] The algorithm used in non-custodian wallets would fall under both categories. It takes over from humans in MLFT detection. However, the investigation and final decision to prosecute remains with the FIU. The use of AI to take over part of the human process is an argument for a comprehensive legal identity, some argue even beyond that of normal humans.[71] Treating the non-custodian wallet as a separate entity offers some opportunities. Thereby raising the question of what legal personality should be granted.

5.5 Classification of Digital Personality

The approach to awarding full legal personality entails the award of potential liability to the algorithm. In order to compensate for potential damages the algorithm would need resources. This could be achieved either through a minimum level of funds in a bank account or through insurance.[72] This approach theoretically works in the case of a self-driving vehicle. I.e. a self-driving bus service could pay for such

---

[65] Cerka et al. (2017), p. 689.

[66] Ibid.

[67] Sjöberg (2020), p. 84.

[68] See; article 59(f) European Parliament resolution of 16 February 2017 with recommendations to the Commission on Civil Law Rules on Robotics (2015/2103(INL)).

[69] Van Eerten and Van Heugten (2018).

[70] Gaivoronskaya et al. (2021), p. 1137.

[71] Cerka et al. (2017).

[72] Schirmer (2020), p. 131.

insurance automatically through the passenger fees. Each time a passenger uses the service a percentage of their ticket could automatically flow to the insurance company. This type of system would not require a connection between the producer and the intelligent machine after creation. The question is whether this would work with non-custodian wallets. In order for such a system to work the non-custodian wallet would have to generate an income whereby automatically (part of) the revenues flow to an insurance company. These revenues could be made through transaction fees or paid advertisements. In case of contested liability, legal representation could occur through the insurance company. The algorithm would have a full legal personality but is represented through its insurance. Though a full legal personality would solve various issues it does not fit within the legal framework.

Full legal personality can be based upon either natural persons or legal persons. Both of these personalities are based upon either rational persons or a company represented by rational and responsive directors. The main argument against basing the legal personhood is that the AI would hold human rights.[73] This argument is, however, not true. The holding of human rights is often limited to what we consider "full humans". In the course of history slaves, women and minorities have not held (all) human rights. Nevertheless, we associate natural persons with the ideas of humans and humanity.[74] AI is not a human and is not directly comparable with natural persons. Even though the rights associated with being a person can be limited, the rationale is off. The next option for a full legal personality is that of legal personhood. The type of personality given to companies. The legal person would then be the AI which is represented through its directors. In this case that would be either the developer or the supervisor. In case of a dispute between the insurance company and the algorithm, the developer or supervisor will be considered the addressee. In case of a dispute over pricing with the insurer, the wallet will have to be represented by its developer. Though this type of personality fits better than the figure of natural personhood, it is not exactly right either. The director(s) of a firm are considered to act on behalf of the firm and to have control over the firm. Neither the supervisor nor the developer has full control over the algorithm's decision-making. To award full legal personality to the algorithm is therefore a bridge too far. One answer might therefore be to consider the wallet and its algorithm subject to a set of limited rights and rules.[75] One such approach involves examining the non-custodian wallet through the principal-agency theory.

To construct a form of semi-legal personality the principal-agency theory can be applied.[76] Whereby the algorithmic entity, in this case the non-custodian wallet, is considered the agent that is given its mandate through coding. The agent has a set of duties and is considered separate but attached to the principal. This theory applied to

---

[73] Open letter to the European Commission Artificial Intelligence and Robotics, available on: http://www.robotics-openletter.eu/.
[74] Bennet and Daly (2020), pp. 65–66.
[75] Schirmer (2020), p. 131.
[76] Andrade et al. (2007), pp. 357–373.

the non-custodian wallet, offers various opportunities for supervision. The algorithm can be considered subject to quality standards. The developer can be held liable for the malfunctioning of the algorithm due to wrongful programming. Providing such a legal personality would furthermore enable the agents to cooperate with each other.[77] Whilst this creates a situation whereby there is some separation between the creation phase and monitoring phase, there are some issues. As mentioned earlier it is not always easy to spot why an algorithm has malfunctioned, nor is it always a fault within programming. The principal-agent theory furthermore assumes an agent capable of human aspects, such as moral awareness and free will.[78] The framework furthermore relies upon two parties. The first is the principal who provides the instructions and the second is the agent who executes these instructions. The algorithm within the non-custodian wallet would however receive input from the developer and the supervisor. The principal-agent theory is therefore not suitable as a legal framework for non-custodian wallets. There are different ways other than principal-agent theory to regulate algorithmic entities. An interesting take upon the partial-legal personality is that of the German teilrechtsfähigkeit.

The "teilrechtsfähigkeit" approach is one whereby a person or entity only has half a legal personality.[79] The rights and duties are granted based upon a functional approach, whereby those rights and duties that are needed are awarded.[80] In this case, the non-custodial wallet would be given the duty to be based upon a supervisor-approved algorithm. With the right and duty to take insurance against damage claims. The wallet would have a form of civil law responsibility and if so desired could have criminal liability too. The wallet software could be given fines in case of malfunction. The question, however, is whether this is desirable when the wallet neither intends to malfunction nor its instructions are based upon input from other legal entities. The free will, upon which our criminal justice system is based, is not present within algorithms. Criminal liability is therefore not a duty to be placed upon AI. Private liability for damages on the other hand can be partially awarded to an algorithm. Damages under private law can have two motives. The compensatory damages aim to compensate a victim and the punitive damages aim to punish the wrongdoer. The AI should be awarded the duty to pay compensatory damages, but not punitive damages. Punitive damages are a civil law form of punishment and should not be awarded as the AI lacks free will. The content duties and responsibilities should be awarded by the law. These duties and rights would need to allow for the creation of a non-custodian wallet that can be supervised. Whereby the duties mirror those of the custodian supervisors.

The difficulty of removing human interaction is the right to an explanation, whereby third parties have a right to know why their transaction is considered suspicious. This right was mentioned earlier in relation to simple algorithms. Simple

---

[77] Ibid.
[78] Schirmer (2020), p. 126.
[79] Ibid, pp. 135–136.
[80] Ibid, pp. 135–136.

5.5 Classification of Digital Personality

algorithms can be explained by the user and the user is generally responsible for publishing the data that was entered into the algorithm and the decisions that were made.[81] The complex algorithms that would be used for non-custodian wallets would not be easy to explain. In particular, because there is not one party that inserts the data or understands the algorithm after it has started self-learning. The algorithm would therefore have to be able to explain itself. This type of system is difficult to generate but it is not impossible. A new generation of algorithms is being developed. This type of algorithm is XAI whereby the algorithm is programmed to develop and consider constitutional values.[82] Strides towards human explanations from algorithms are made,[83] thus increasing the possibility of an algorithm that can fulfil the duty of explaining its decision-making. The concept of a 'black box' is real but increasingly algorithms can avoid creating an impenetrable system. The right to an explanation should furthermore not be confused with the right to a simple explanation. A local court in The Netherlands therefore stated that the right to an explanation included that the defense or an expert could inspect the data.[84] The continued development of AI and increased complexity may require experts to interpret and explain the data and coding.[85] Furthermore, the risk of avoiding the supervisory framework is also real. Not only criminals will try and avoid supervision. Avoiding customer identification will form an easier and less costly process for customers. Considering the speed and easiness of transferring currency through the Metaverse, it would be unwise to leave a category of wallets unregulated. Creating legislation that focuses on digital entities would be the most resilient. The concept of what constitutes different entities is flexible and hence can adapt as technology advances.

By regulating non-custodian wallets through their algorithms, monitoring is increased. The additional legislation reduces the potential for money laundering but it risks pushing smaller providers out of the markets through the increased regulation. The resulting limited supply might generate fewer choices for consumers. Thus preventing optimal development of the market. To avoid such a situation from occurring a third category should be added to the regulatory framework. In addition to the custodian and the non-custodian wallet with a monitoring algorithm, the law should identify the supervised anonymous wallet (SA-wallet). The SA-wallet could be constructed using similar legislation as is currently used for anonymous general-purpose prepaid cards. The AMLD5 considers that whilst these cards have their use, they are highly vulnerable to MLFT. General purpose cards with a non-EU origin, are only accepted when they abide by an MLFT framework with similar standards to those of the EU.[86] It is therefore recommended to place limits upon anonymous wallets. The incorporation of anonymous wallets into the legal framework, however,

---

[81] See for example: RvS 17 mei 2017, ECLI:NL:RVS:2017:1259: parafs. 14.3–14.4.
[82] See: Arrieta et al. (2020), pp. 82–115.
[83] Byrne (2019).
[84] Rb Rotterdam 21 september 2021, ECLI:NL:RBROT:2021:9086, paraf. 112.
[85] Kim and Routledge (2022), pp. 75–102.
[86] See preambles 14 and 15.

does require supervision. The supervisor would be responsible for assessing the wallet's limits and adding them to their list of supervised entities.

This approach would enable an exhaustive supervisory framework that allows various wallet structures to exist with supervision. Nevertheless, the EU can only generate such a framework for those wallets offering services from or within the EU jurisdiction. The problem is that consumers can quite easily use wallets from outside the EU jurisdiction. To limit the use of unsupervised wallets the EU can use the Internet of Things.

5.6 Jurisdiction on Transactions Made to Third-Countries

The Metaverse will incorporate a wide array of wallets which will be located in various jurisdictions. These transactions can increase international trade and competition. The ease by which wallets from various jurisdictions can be used however also carries the risk of rule avoidance. As discussed in Sect. 4.4.2 this can occur through forum-shopping of providers by choosing low-regulated jurisdictions. Or by avoiding choosing a jurisdiction altogether and operating in full anonymity.

Currently, the AMLD5 approaches this issue by applying the legislation to those offering their services from or in the EU. This system aims to regulate the wallets within the EU and thereby the currencies flowing in and out of the EU. This system is theoretically sound but practically generates two risks. The first risk is the broad definition of offering services to the various Member States. There are some guidelines to determine whether a service is offered within the Member States.[87] These guidelines are wide and open to discussion. In particular, in Member States where English is widely, but not officially, spoken a piece of software can be used without it being officially offered in the state. It is important to consider therefore that a wallet can be easily accessed and installed globally even when not specifically offered to a certain market. Therefore the EU system will not be able to regulate all wallets accessible within the internal market. Secondly, such an approach does not discuss how to consider a transaction between regulated wallets and those whereby the jurisdiction cannot be established. When transferring funds to another bank account the jurisdiction is established through the physical location of the bank. This is often identified through the bank account's International Bank Account Number (IBAN). Whilst there are several such numbers used internationally, the identification of the bank and the jurisdiction is relatively easy. Software wallets are not required to carry jurisdiction identification numbers. Thus raising the question of how to regulate transactions to such wallets. The combination of accessibility and un-identifiability creates serious holes in the current legislative approach. These gaps can be mitigated if wallets are considered as things within the Internet of Things.

---

[87] CJEU 7 December 2010 (*Pammer v Schlüter and Hotel Alpenhof v. Heller*) ECLI:EU:C:2010: 740.

5.6 Jurisdiction on Transactions Made to Third-Countries

The IoT refers to a system of objects that can be physical, virtual or hybrid which can communicate with each other to facilitate various system functions.[88] The entities within the IoT network can communicate and receive data from each other. The communication between entities allows for impact assessment of transactions. It can provide assistance in preventing MLFT and consumer protection to an extent that is yet to be explored in the financial system. To avoid risky transactions the wallet of the sender would need to be able to establish to whom the receiving wallet belongs, where that person is physically located and under what jurisdiction the wallet is regulated. This can be implemented to warn consumers when there is a likelihood of a scam. For example, a Somali pirate (wallet A) tries to provoke a consumer (wallet B) to transfer money by pretending to be a relative.[89] Wallet A sends a transaction request to wallet B. In response to receiving this request, wallet B asks for further details such as location. Wallet A can verify its own location through the device's GPS or a specific app and work as a tracker. The entity (Wallet A) on the tracker transmits this data to Wallet B. Wallet B upon receiving the information that Wallet A is accessed from Somalia (or has no location) considers that the transaction is suspicious and warns its owner to not engage in the transaction. A second form of implementation is to avoid transactions between high and low-regulated jurisdictions. For example, a wallet supervised by the Dutch supervisor could engage in a transaction with a wallet supervised by the French supervisor but not with a non-supervised or poorly supervised wallet. The technology to facilitate such communications and transactions is available.[90] This type of communication is not only possible but already occurs between other things communicating via the internet. The strategy on how to regulate such wallets can therefore be mirrored upon the Internet of Things (IoT). The question is how to regulate the wallets as part of the IoT.

The IoT is not extensively regulated in the EU. In 2009 the Commission identified 14 points of action.[91] Despite this early communication, legislative action has been limited. In 2018 a Directive was published that included the IoT, the Directive concerned the use and allocation of radio communication.[92] More recently in 2021, the IoT was mentioned once on the EU's strategic research agenda.[93] In 2022 the Commission published its sectoral report on the IoT which focused on

---

[88] Ray (2018), pp. 291–319.

[89] A scheme based upon a con-trick that resurfaces in different variations.

[90] Saia et al. (2019), pp. 77–84.

[91] Communication from the commission to the European Parliament, the Council, the European Economic and Social Committee and the Committee of the Regions Internet of Things — An action plan for Europe, Brussels 18 June 2009 COM(2009) 278.

[92] Directive (EU) 2018/1972 of the European Parliament and of the Council of 11 December 2018 establishing the European Electronic Communications Code.

[93] Decision (EU) 2021/820 of the European Parliament and of the Council of 20 May 2021 on the Strategic Innovation Agenda of the European Institute of Innovation and Technology (EIT) 2021–2027: Boosting the Innovation Talent and Capacity of Europe and repealing Decision No 1312/2013/EU.

various aspects, in particular competition.[94] The EU approach on how to regulate the entities, however, is not yet defined. There are several approaches possible to regulate the IoT. The first is that of anarchy.

The anarchist approach favours bottom-up regulation. The regulation would ideally, according to anarchism, form organically through network cooperation.[95] Wachhaus describes that the IoT will shape in different networks which are hard to detect by a central institution.[96] His vision is that the networks will be able to organize themselves through clear communication and common goals.[97] Using his approach to successfully implement an anarchistic approach to governance and regulation thus requires communication and common goals. When considering the entities that can be used for payment in the Metaverse these can likely communicate very clearly. The entities are designed to be able to communicate and transact with each other. Furthermore, there appears to be a common goal, namely to conduct efficient global transactions. Thus creating a theoretically strong argument to use an anarchist approach to regulate digital payment entities. Prima facie this regulatory approach seems to be supported by economic theory. Coase argued that under certain circumstances the ideal outcome concerning externalities will be reached, without relying on government intervention.[98] His theory takes the example of pollution and a factory, but more scenarios may apply. In the case of wallets, the negative externality would be the increased risk of MLFT through regulation. The latter is indicated by the tendency of various financial institutes to locate in low-tax and low-regulatory jurisdictions.[99] Whilst consumer users will wish for a safe system, firms may focus on efficient and low-cost systems. The ideal outcome would be a system that is regulated and monitored to prevent MLFT from occurring. For the anarchist approach to work, the networks have to be able to regulate themselves. According to Coase, this would be possible when the transaction costs are negligible. Theoretically, these costs are low as communication between digital entities is cheap and easy. As the earlier example of a potential Somali pirate demonstrates the wallets can communicate with ease. The information provided to the consumer can then help the consumer in estimating the risks and acting accordingly. In theory, the consumer would reject any risky transactions and only transact with (well) regulated wallets. In theory therefore those with savory intentions would opt to use well-regulated wallets. The theory, however, is unlike to meet reality.

---

[94] Regulation (EU) 2019/881 of the European Parliament and of the Council of 17 April 2019 on ENISA (the European Union Agency for Cybersecurity) and on information and communications technology cybersecurity certification and repealing Regulation (EU) No 526/2013 (Cybersecurity Act).
[95] Wachhaus (2011), p. 36.
[96] Ibid, p. 38.
[97] Ibid.
[98] Hurwicz (1995), p. 74.
[99] See Sect. 3.3.2.

The reality is that communication between digital entities will likely be strong. This, however, does not mean a user has all the needed information. If we assume that a user wishes to install a safe software wallet, the user requires knowledge of what level of regulation and safety checks apply to the wallets. This means the customer will have to research the regulatory framework applicable to its own wallet. Furthermore, any well-regulated wallet will require customer verification. Thus increasing the effort needed from the consumer in order to use the software. When transacting the user will receive communication from the other party's wallet. The information, however, may include what regulatory framework is applicable to the software but not how strong the regulatory framework is. The user will then have to research whether it considers this regulatory framework safe. The need to research the regulatory framework indicates a discrepancy of information between the parties. The user is thereby forced to either accept the risk or spend resources researching the system. The transaction costs of Coase's theorem are therefore not negligible. This is even more so if the options for the consumer are low. The result would be for the consumer either not to conduct the transaction or accept the risk. If the consumer chooses to accept the risks the consequent externality is that of a higher MLFT risk. The tendency of businesses to locate in less regulated jurisdictions therefore decreases the chances of a successful governance system based on anarchism. The unregulated economy would then outgrow the regulated economy, whilst the opposite is intended. Coase's theorem furthermore included the use of government-regulated systems when needed.[100] The current EU approach whereby the EU regulates the EU territory as a single public body does not seem to work either. A middle ground should be introduced. Weber introduces an approach based on regulation through multiple stakeholders.

The proposal made by Weber is to approach the IoT through a 'multi-stakeholder in governance'.[101] In this approach, there are multiple regulatory entities which are decentralized and consider the needs of all stakeholders.[102] This approach can largely be identified in the current AML framework. Whereby the rules are harmonized at the EU level. Nevertheless, various entities contribute to the governance and implementation of these rules. These entities include national supervisors and supranational bodies such as the FATF and Commission who identify specific risks. With regard to the Metaverse, the multi-stakeholder approach seems the most inclusive and efficient. The national supervisors can collaborate to create a European virtual compliance certificate. Thus replacing the current registration in all Member States with a virtual European Passport (as is custom with other financial service providers). To maximize efficiency, however, stakeholder selection would need to include private parties such as reality and wallet providers.

The stakeholders that could be allowed a seat at the table in this network approach are the large Metaverse reality providers. It is not unlikely that some Metaverse

---

[100] Weber (2009), pp. 522–527.
[101] Ibid: 526.
[102] Ibid.

realities will be more popular than others. The realities that operate with large volumes of transactions and/or users should be allowed a voice in this network. They can contribute to the risk identification assessments and even be allowed to apply for supervisory status. Let us consider an example whereby a Metaverse reality consists of a large international shopping street with various traders from different jurisdictions. This Metaverse reality could function as a universally accessible shopping street like the Dutch PC Hoofdstraat or French Champs-Élysées. The primary difference is that the shops are not registered in a single jurisdiction, nor is their jurisdiction clear due to the lack of a physical location. A virtual customer could purchase a high-priced item through various anonymous wallets. The cash equivalent of the transaction would have to be reported by the shop owner. In the Metaverse such reporting duties will often be unclear. The virtual reality provider could in such cases act as the monitoring entity where suspicious transactions have to be reported. The reality provider could operate as a liaison with the national supervisor. Furthermore, the reality provider could be awarded supervisory duties to ensure unregulated wallets cannot engage with its environment. Engaging with private parties would enable the regulators to identify which environments are deemed 'safe'. The supervisor could in response provide a digital certificate confirming that the environment complies with the safety standards of the EU. A similar approach could be used towards wallet providers.

The Commission has identified countries with high MLFT risks. Wallets regulated under these jurisdictions should thus be considered risky. The consequence however is that wallet providers in these jurisdictions have less opportunity to compete with highly regulated jurisdictions. Thus excluding them from the virtual market. This exclusion can be accepted but that does not seem fair. The EU could design an opt-in strategy whereby these providers can opt into the EU's regulatory framework. The most logical opt-in supervisor would be the newly proposed EU AML Supervisory Authority.[103] This authority will be responsible for AML supervision at the EU level. The potential disadvantage is a high number of individual providers who would wish to register. Particularly when individual parties wish to opt in. Rather, however, the EU could work with a system whereby it delegates that responsibility and allows for private parties to provide such certification. The EU AML Authority then strictly supervise the private parties providing the certificates. Whilst the governance approach is generally laudable there are two difficulties with this approach.

The multi-stakeholder approach requires a new way of thinking about regulation.[104] In particular, the network approach is ahead of the law. The law has not yet caught up with the network approach.[105] For this system to be successful the law has

---

[103] Proposal for a Regulation of the European Parliament and of the Council establishing the Authority for Anti-Money Laundering and Countering the Financing of Terrorism and amending Regulations (EU) No 1093/2010, (EU) 1094/2010, (EU) 1095/2010.

[104] Weber (2009), p. 526.

[105] Zouridis and Leijtens (2021), pp. 118–129.

to assign clear responsibilities to the parties involved. Governance within the current EU Economic and Monetary Union (EMU) functions under the threat of the law.[106] Thus ensuring that parties are obliged to take their task seriously or risk judicial sanctions.[107] Judicial sanctions, however, require a clear assignment of obligations. To regulate the network governance, the law will have to provide clear standards and potential liabilities and/or punishments if these standards are not met.[108] These standards in combination with serious actors could monitor and regulate the Metaverse economy. The standards, however, need developing. The second difficulty is the question of whether consumers should be prevented from transacting with unregulated wallets. Thus creating the distinction between wallets that are registered with a supervisor and those that are not. To promote the use of supervised wallets. The law could require registered wallets only to allow the execution of transactions with registered wallets. This rule would be written into the software coding of the wallet in order to be registered with a supervisor. De facto this creates a closed economy only accessible through supervised entities. The non-registered wallets could either opt to be registered or operate outside the EU only. As these wallets could still be downloaded, though the use could be prohibited, it risks creating two payment systems.

Creating two economies is not ideal. Nevertheless, there is currently already a system of two economies in place due to the differentiation of custodian and non-custodian wallets. Furthermore by creating a fully regulated system consumers can enjoy the protection of regulation. The question is whether consumers should be mandated to use the system. If there is no legal obligation for consumers to use the regulated system, they should do so voluntarily. For consumers to use the regulated system they will have to judge using the regulated system as more valuable than the unregulated system. There are various arguments to consider that the consumer would opt for the regulated wallet. The first argument resides in the moral judgement of the consumer. There are different shades of grey when considering the informal economy. A consumer will have a different moral attitude towards human trafficking than towards informal labour.[109] If the regulated wallet is trusted to prevent MLFT this would nudge the consumer towards its use. Similar observations can be made with regard to fair trade labels. Consumers are willing to purchase and consume responsibly.[110] Nevertheless, there is also evidence that it also depends on the personal values of the consumer.[111] The use of ethical purchasing is therefore not a guarantee of success. Additionally, consumers do not always purchase ethically despite their intentions. This phenomenon is called the 'intention-behavior gap',

---

[106] Dawson (2011), p. 83.

[107] Ibid.

[108] It is beyond the scope of this contribution to examine the content of the legislation, for suggestions see: Tzafestas (2018), pp. 98–120; Almeida et al. (2015), pp. 56–59.

[109] Hinterseer (2002), p. 71.

[110] Shaw and Newholm (2002), pp. 167–185.

[111] Ladhari and Tchetgna (2015), pp. 469–477.

behavioural economists are currently unsure as to why this phenomenon takes place.[112] Hence nudging based on ethical considerations may not be effective enough. Stronger regulation by excluding non-regulated wallets is therefore required.

The second argument that registered wallets would generate more consumption, however, is trust. Consumers may trust regulated technology more than non-regulated technology. The higher level of consumer protection would therefore assist in pushing the non-regulated wallets into decline. There is, however, the argument here that cryptocurrencies were invented to avoid regulated institutions. Thus reducing the likelihood that consumers will prefer to use a regulated wallet. Nevertheless, there is good reason to believe consumers will not opt for safety. In particular when the risk of fraud or MLFT is wrongly estimated. Based on privacy and car insurance, Bailey considers this underestimating the risks that apply to the consumers' perception of IoT.[113] Consumers overestimate their control over their own driving behaviour and subsequently underestimate the risk of sharing their monitored driving information.[114] Considering the wrongful estimation of risks there is a strong argument to protect the consumer from harm. Additionally, Bailey continues by indicating consumers prefer a purchase today over higher future costs. Privacy concerns in the future are thereby estimated as a lower concern than the use of technology today. In particular with IoT, the negative consequences are not certain.[115] One solution to these issues according to Bailey is the mandatory disclosure.[116] Disclosure of the risky transaction through the wallets is possible before the transaction is executed. Nevertheless, this disclosure does not work reducing consumers' optimism.[117] The second legal solution is requiring explicit consent for the risk from the consumer. This is the so-called opt-in system rather than opt-out.[118] Whereby a consumer has to specifically agree to take a certain risk. The explicit consent would be integrated into the wallet system. The consumer will have to verify that it wishes to make the transaction after receiving the information from the counterparty's device. Nevertheless, it is questionable whether this system is secure enough to prevent MLFT. Consumers will remain overly optimistic and likely to make a purchase. Bailey considers that limiting the consumers' options through legislation would be heavy-handed. It would reduce rational consumers' choices and would prevent consumers from learning from their mistakes.[119] Whilst these are potentially correct with regard to privacy issues these arguments are less appropriate in the case of MLFT. The outcomes of a violation of the consumer's privacy would

---

[112] Hassan et al. (2014), pp. 219–236.
[113] Bailey (2015–2016), p. 1037.
[114] Ibid.
[115] Ibid, p. 1040.
[116] Ibid, p. 1041.
[117] Ibid.
[118] Ibid, pp. 1045–1046.
[119] Ibid, pp. 1052–1053.

be harmful to the consumer involved. However, MLFT carries externalities beyond that of the individual consumer. Furthermore, violence is often associated with gun and drug sales but not the financial system that facilitated MLFT.

The third nudging option is for governments to promote the use of regulated wallets by their own adoption. Governments transact only through regulated virtual wallets and mandate businesses located within their jurisdiction to do the same. If businesses and the government use regulated wallets, consumers will be forced into using regulated wallets. Whilst technically possible this risks the same issue as previously considered with the current regulatory approach. Governments can influence businesses on their territory. However, the current global trade would provide ample opportunity for consumers to purchase products from or through lesser-regulated jurisdictions. Thus such an approach would not be a likely solution. The fourth option to nudge consumers into using a regulated wallet is by using criminal law. Rather than directly prohibition the regulatory wallets the government could deem any transaction suspicious and the consumer will have to prove the transaction was not suspicious. This solution is close to prohibiting the non-regulated wallets and is not perfect either. In particular, because it would entail a huge burden upon the FIU and criminal justice system. The more effective option is therefore to prohibit the use of unsupervised software wallets. This creates a legal framework that is largely regulated, though avoiding regulation is nearly always possible. It does not solve the second issue associated with the Metaverse and placement namely that of smurfing through smart contracts.

5.7 Smart Contracts

The previous paragraphs have discussed the reduction of anonymity when placing funds into the Metaverse. Whilst anonymity is the largest risk associated with the placement phase it is not the only one. Another important issue is the existence of smart contracts that can be built into the Metaverse. Smart contracts are contracts that operate automatically without the need for intermediaries. An example of a basic smart contract is that of a vending machine. Whereby you pay €2,00 and the machine gives you the beverage (and change if needed). The transaction occurs fully automatically without the need for the beverage sales agent to be present. A smart contract is built upon a blockchain and written in coding language. These contracts are created in environments that facilitate writing smart contracts. The code for a smart contract is rather particular and can be found in special 'coding dictionaries' such as Java Script or Solidity. After writing (and testing) these contracts can be connected to the wallets and deployed via the blockchain. Smart contracts can be used within the Metaverse if they are written in code compatible with EVM bytecode. The latter is compatible with the largest coding dictionary currently available. It is therefore a reasonable assumption that smart contracts will be used in the Metaverse. Whilst the use of smart contracts is still limited, these contracts can facilitate and improve the efficiency of trade. Despite their advantages, smart

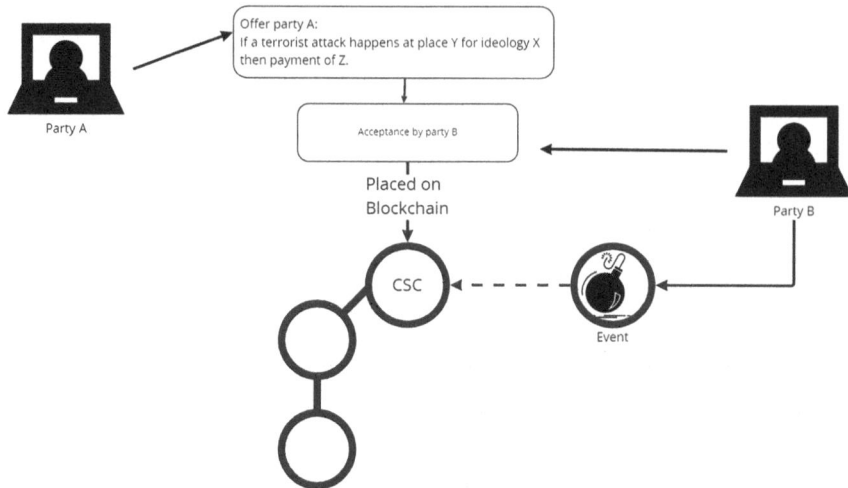

Fig. 5.3 Criminal smart contract for the financing of terrorism

contracts can also reduce the effort needed to commit financial crimes. There are two different risks that smart contracts pose. The first is the smart contracts that facilitate crimes.

The first category is those smart contracts that offer payment in return for criminal activity. These types of contracts can include the sale of trade secrets or the promise of payment for a murder. The smart contract can facilitate the arrangement of criminal activity without trust. A normal contract requires the parties to trust each other. If a person pays for a terrorist event to take place and the other party does not execute, the person paying cannot go to court. Because a judge will likely convict the claimant for financing terrorism.[120] Within the world of criminal smart contracts (CSC), trust is no longer necessary. Instead, the CSC is negotiated and once accepted placed upon the blockchain. Once on the blockchain, the CSC cannot be altered. The CSC will execute payment automatically when it is told the event has taken place. When the CSC gains the confirmation that the crime has been committed it will send payment to the agreed executer. The automatic payment reduces the need to trust the opposing party. These CSCs are technically feasible and a realistic threat.[121] The difficulty at present is to connect smart contracts to a trusted external source that informs the CSC that the event has taken place. A smart contract that promises payment in return for terrorist activity would look as demonstrated in Fig. 5.3.

The figure demonstrates a simple smart contract for financing terrorist activity. It shows that an anonymous party can offer a payment in return for an attack. The second party (Party B) can accept the terms. The contract then moves on to the blockchain and will automatically pay Party B when the event has been finalized.

---

[120] E.g. in the Dutch criminal code such practice is prohibited by article 421.
[121] Juels et al. (2016).

5.7 Smart Contracts

The problem at present is how to record the event on the blockchain. A blockchain only approves an event to its chain when all nodes consider the event to have happened. Since not all nodes (computers running the blockchain) will process the event at the same time, little deviations may occur. These deviations cause the event to be denied on the blockchain. It is however only a matter of time before this problem is solved. There are already services that provide (accurate) external information, such as weather events, to the blockchain called Oracles. These services will likely expand to include external events. A terrorist CSC is therefore only a matter of time.

The second category of smart contracts is when the smart contract is used to commit a crime. As discussed in Chap. 4, funds are generally placed within the system through a process called 'smurfing'. This process entails placing a high volume of low sum values into the system to avoid detection. Placing these funds into the system can be done manually by placing small funds into different wallets or by placing small funds into the same wallet over time. The manual effort needed to place the funds into the wallet(s) can be replaced by a smart contract. Smart contracts can furthermore be used to execute transactions in order to layer the funds placed into the system. Smurfing is a technique that is conducted to prevent detection from supervisors. The need to avoid detection will increase when the anonymity of wallets is lifted (or at least seriously decreased). The question is therefore how to supervise and detect CSCs.

Despite the current innovation in smart contracts, the legislation has not yet been updated to the extent necessary. There is some argument that CSCs are unlikely to succeed.[122] The likelihood of a successful conclusion of a CSC was based upon a contract to leak information. This contract would be hindered by unreliable initiators and the freeriding problem. Consumers would wait until other consumers had purchased the goods and thereby released the information.[123] These factors play a reduced role in financing terrorism or smurfing. The CSCs would only have two wallets connected. The free-rider problem is therefore much lower.

The Commission has commissioned a report on regulating blockchains and smart contracts.[124] The report, however, does not specifically address smart contracts for criminal activities. The CSCs themselves are likely to be illegal in most countries. National criminal codes are unlikely to distinguish between a physical agreement and a digital agreement to commit a crime. Criminalizing an activity, however, is fruitless without proper monitoring and policing. There is currently no set plan from the EU to monitor smart contracts within the framework of MLFT. There are, however, several approaches possible to monitoring and regulating smart contracts. There are four phases in the life span of a smart contract. The first is the creation of

---

[122] Wang et al. (2019), pp. 291–301.

[123] Ibid.

[124] Legal and regulatory framework of blockchains and smart contracts. The European Union Blockchain observatory and forum. (2019) available at: https://www.eublockchainforum.eu/sites/default/files/reports/report_legal_v1.0.pdf.

the contract, the second is the freezing, the third is execution and the fourth is the finalization.[125]

A smart contract is created through coding, using a coding language. This coding language is generated by tech firms in the form of a complex coding dictionary. A logical first step would be to prohibit any coding language that allows the creation of CSCs. The language of 'terrorist' or 'attack' could be prohibited. This type of approach would prevent such contracts from the ability to be drafted. Whilst technically possible it would not solve the problem and create more difficulties. Firstly the coding language can be replaced by using different words. Secondly, such an approach creates difficulty in drafting insurance contracts. What if a smart insurance policy wishes to include or exclude a terrorist attack? The third difficulty is that in the case of money laundering, placing small amounts of money into the Metaverse through a smart contract is not illegal by itself. A contract that states that every x amount of time y amount of money should be transferred, is not inherently for unsavoury intentions. The illegality of smurfing is through its intention to launder money. It is therefore not recommended to prohibit the coding of structuring contracts. Such a prohibition would risk prohibiting any code that entails payment of a long-term contract. Regulating the coding language therefore does not seem like a valid option. The next part within the first stage of the CSC is the offering and acceptance phase. Hereby a CSC offer would be placed on an illegal market and accepted before it is placed upon the blockchain. Whilst it is the most appropriate place to supervise it is certainly difficult. It would entail a supervisory duty upon each marketplace. The marketplace for such contracts is unlikely to be compliant with such duties. This supervision is furthermore within the realm of criminal code which is beyond the scope of this book.

The second phase of a smart contract is that of the freeze phase.[126] During this phase, the CSC is verified by the nodes and deployed to the blockchain. It is difficult to regulate this phase in the smart contract's life cycle. The nodes verify the information but do not form a monitoring function. It would currently be very difficult to find a system to have these nodes form a monitoring function. The programs used to deploy a smart contract to the blockchain can be regulated. These programs allow a user to create a smart contract, test it and place it on the blockchain. The testing of a smart contract occurs through modelling. The modelling can test whether a smart contract is secure and functional.[127] These modelling techniques can be adapted to include a risk assessment for MLFT. The program would check the contract before deployment to establish whether the contract is likely used for MLFT. It could then prohibit the contract from being deployed. Though it would be an effective approach these deployment programmes could likely be avoided. It would furthermore reduce the speed of deploying smart contracts. It is nevertheless advisable to bring such programmes under the scope

---

[125] Sillaber and Waltl (2017), pp. 498–499.
[126] Ibid, p. 499.
[127] Almakhour et al. (2020), pp. 1–19.

5.7 Smart Contracts

of AML legislation. Partially because it reduces the possibility of generating anonymous smart contracts. Secondly setting technological standards for preventing MLFT, decreases the possibility of creating CSCs through the accepted platforms.

The third phase is when the blockchain receives the information that the event has taken place. To prohibit the blockchain from receiving information on terrorist attacks is a difficult approach. One approach is to decrease the likeliness of the accuracy of the external data reaching the CSCs. These technologies are in their early development but do show promise.[128] Such approaches would reduce the likelihood of successful implementation of the CSCs. The approach, however, focuses on the smart contract itself rather than the person or people behind the smart contract. Therefore even if such techniques were used to decrease the effectiveness of CSCs, a supervisory strategy to detect the criminals behind the contract is still needed. Detecting the person(s) behind the CSC is possible through the contact between the wallet and the CSC.

The fourth phase is that of finalization, in this phase, the payment is provided. The previous paragraphs considered the supervisory powers of the wallet. The CSC for calling card crimes such as the organization of a terrorist attack also need to communicate with a wallet. The first approach would be to consider transactions coming in after an attack has been reported to the wallet, as suspicious. This approach, however, includes everyone who receives insurance payouts or an unrelated payment briefly after an attack. It furthermore as a method is focused on finding the attacker after the event, rather than before. The supervisor intends to prevent attacks from taking place. With regard to the smurfing contracts, a duty of notice can be introduced.

Currently, financial institutions have to conduct an investigation when a transaction or a combination of transactions reaches a threshold. A similar duty can be introduced for wallets with regard to smart contracts. A smart contract reaching a combined threshold would be investigated. Such legislation would closely follow the current legislation for banking. Furthermore, a smart contract that is concluded for legitimate reasons would remain possible. Though technically possible and closely mimicking the other legislation, this system is not foolproof. Smurfing through regular payment accounts takes effort. The effort is still highly reduced through the use of smart contracts and criminals may use multiple smart contracts to remain out of sight. Nevertheless, the reporting rule would be an excellent start.

In general, legislation to monitor and supervise MLFT should target the first and last stages of the smart contract. In the first and last phases, the wallets are used to communicate. These wallets are connected to the people who intend to commit MLFT. The freezing stage can be targeted through the deployment mechanism. This would however target the entering of the freezing stage rather than the verification from the nodes itself. The third phase is that of the blockchain. When the CSC is placed on the blockchain it will be difficult to regulate. Though there are techniques

---

[128] Zhang et al. (2019), pp. 144–153.

to reduce proper finalization, these are policing techniques rather than monitoring and supervisory issues.

5.8 Conclusion and Recommendations

The first difficulty when considering MLFT and the Metaverse is the variety of wallets available. The wallets can be generated either on their own or as part of a variety of services. The wide variety means that for a legislative response to be effective it should cover all forms of wallets. The EU approach uses the term entity to describe the wallet provider. This term is considerably broad and therefore unlikely to distinguish between pure wallets and wallets offered as part of a package. More difficult, however, is the regulatory exclusion of non-custodian wallets.

Non-custodian wallets have been excluded from the regulatory framework. Non-custodian wallets are wallets sold as a product rather than a service. Therefore the developer is gone once the product has been sold. This does not fit with the current legislative approach that focuses on human supervision. The focus on human supervision, however, is outdated. Even in other areas of the financial sector human supervision is largely replaced with algorithms. Humans only filter the outcomes of the algorithm. This filtering job sounds important but as it turns out the number of false positives remains rather high despite human intervention. To make an algorithm directly responsible for supervision is therefore a realistic alternative. The algorithm can be built into the non-custodian wallet and directly communicate with the national FIU. To make such a system successful the national supervisor has to develop standards of algorithmic efficiency. This allows for a fair judgement of algorithms before they enter the market. Secondly, a system of accountability for mistakes should be developed. This accountability should be created along with a new legal personality for digital entities. To shift focus on the quality of algorithms and other aspects of technology is scary to any legislator. Nevertheless, this shift would allow for non-custodian wallets to be part of the regulated framework, rather than form their own unregulated market.

A further step towards embracing technology into the regulatory framework is by developing the Internet of Things. A system in which things communicate with each other over the internet. By considering wallets as things participating in the IoT more consumer protection can be generated. The wallet can protect its user from possible scams and it can exclude non-regulated wallets. This approach is technically feasible but would require further development of the legislative framework. In particular, the legislator should respond to data protection and protection for the consumer against himself.

In short, the EU legislator has generated a broad framework. The framework, however, is over-reliant on humans. Embracing the use of technology whilst regulating its standards would allow for a more effective supervisory framework against MLFT. This thereby concludes the placement phase of the MLFT in the Metaverse.

As discussed earlier the placement phase is only the first of three phases. The next chapter will therefore continue by discussing the second phase: layering.

References

Almakhour M et al (2020) Verification of smart contracts: a survey. Pervasive Mobile Comp 67: 101227
Almeida V, Doneda D, Monteiro M (2015) Governance challenges for the internet of things. IEEE Internet Comput 19(4):56–59
Andrade F, Novais P, Neves J (2007) Contracting agents: legal personality and representation. Artif Intell Law 15:357–373
Arrieta A et al (2020) Explainable artificial intelligence (XAI): concepts, taxonomies, opportunities and challenges toward responsible AI. Inf Fusion 58:82–115
Azman M, Sharma K (2020) Security of cryptocurrency using hardware wallet and QR code. Proceedings of the Third International Conference on Smart Systems and Inventive Technology (ICSSIT 2020)
Baer T (2019) How real-world biases are mirrored by algorithms. In: Understand, manage, and prevent algorithmic bias. Apress, Berkeley CA
Bailey M (2015) Seduction by technology: why consumers opt out of privacy by buying into the internet of things. Texas Law Rev 94:1023–1054
Beardsley S, Farrell D (2005) Regulation that's good for competition. McKinsey Q 2
Bennet B, Daly A (2020) Recognising rights for robots: can we? Will we? Should we? Law Innov Technol 12(1)
Bikker J, Bos J (2005) Competition and efficiency in banking: international comparisons. Econ Financ Modell
Brownsword R, Somsen H (2009) Law, innovation and technology: before we fast forward – a forum for debate. Law Innov Technol 1(1):1–73
Byrne R (2019) Counterfactuals in explainable Artificial Intelligence (XAI): evidence from human reasoning. Conference Paper available at: https://www.researchgate.net/publication/334844529
Cassella SD (2018) Toward a new model of money laundering. Is the "placement, layering, integration model obsolete?". J Money Laund Control 21
Cerka P, Grigiene J, Sirbikyte G (2017) Is it possible to grant legal personality to artificial intelligence software systems? Comp Law Security Rev 33(5):685–699
Dawson M (2011) New governance and the transformation of European law coordinating EU social law and policy. Cambridge University Press, Cambridge
De Nederlandsche Bank (2020) Leidraad Wwft en Sw. Amsterdam. https://www.dnb.nl/voor-de-sector/open-boek-toezicht/wet-regelgeving/wwft/dnb-leidraad-wwft-en-sw/
Del Monaco S (2020) Money mules and tumblers. Money laundering during the cryptocurrency era. Ricerche giuridiche 9(2)
Edwards L, Veale M (2018) Enslaving the algorithm: from a "right to an explanation" to a "right to better decisions"? IEEE Secur Priv 16(3)
European Banking Authority (2014) Opinion on 'Virtual Currencies'. Frankfurt. https://www.eba.europa.eu/sites/default/documents/files/documents/10180/657547/81409b94-4222-45d7-ba3b-7deb5863ab57/EBA-Op-2014-08%20Opinion%20on%20Virtual%20Currencies.pdf?retry=1
European Central Bank (2020) Report on a digital euro. Frankfurt. Available at: https://www.ecb.europa.eu/pub/pdf/other/Report_on_a_digital_euro~4d7268b458.en.pdf
Fairfield J (2021) Runaway technology. Can the law keep up? Cambridge University Press, Cambridge

Gaivoronskaya Y et al (2021) Logical and conceptual constructions, theoretical and legal versions of the interpretation of the artificial intelligence's "legal personality". Linguistics Culture Rev 5(3)

Gao Z (2009) Application of cluster-based local outlier factor algorithm in anti-money laundering. International Conference on Management and Service Science. https://doi.org/10.1109/ICMSS.2009.5302396

Godlieb A (2018) De vijfde anti-witwasrichtlijn en de potentiële impact op de Europese cryptocurrency-markt. Ondernemingsrecht 101

Haffke L, Fromberger M, Zimmerman P (2019) Cryptocurrencies and anti-money laundering: the shortcomongs of the fifth AML directive (EU) and how to address them. J Bank Regul 21:125–138

Hassan S, De Filippi P (2017) The expansion of algorithmic governance: from code is law to law is code. J Field Actions 17

Hassan L, Shiu E, Shaw D (2014) Who says there is an intention-behaviour gap? Assessing the empirical evidence of an intention-behaviour gap in ethical consumption. J Bus Ethics 136:1–18

Hinterseer K (2002) Criminal finance: the political economy of money laundering in a comparative legal context. Kluwer, The Hague

Howarth J (2022) How many cryptocurrencies are there in 2022. Exploding topics, available at: https://explodingtopics.com/blog/number-of-cryptocurrencies

Hurwicz L (1995) What is the Caose theorem? Jpn World Econ 7(1)

Juels A, Kosba A, Shi E (2016) The Ring of Gyges: investigating the future of criminal smart contracts, Conference on Computer and Communications Security, Vienna 24–28 October 2016

Kannan S, Somasundaram K (2017) Autoregressive-based outlier algorithm to detect money laundering activities. J Money Laund Control 20(2)

Keene S (2012) Emerging threats: financial crime in the virtual world. J Money Laund Control 15(1)

Kelly C, Lynes A (2020) The democratization of white-collar criminality in video games. In: Kelly C, Lynes A (eds) Video games crime and next-gen deviance. Emerald (online)

Kim T, Routledge B (2022) Why a right to an explanation of algorithmic decision-making should exist: a trust-based approach. Bus Ethics Q 32(1)

Köchling A, Wehner M (2020) Discriminated by an algorithm: a systematic review of discrimination and fairness by algorithmic decision-making in the context of HR recruitment and HR development. Bus Res 13

Ladhari R, Tchetgna N (2015) The influence of personal values on fair trade consumption. J Clean Prod 87:469–477

Nederlandse Vereniging van Banken (2019) Nederlandse banken bundelen krachten tegen witwassen. https://www.nvb.nl/nieuws/nederlandse-banken-bundelen-krachten-tegen-witwassen#:~:text=In%20de%20strijd%20tegen%20het,Transactie%20Monitoring%20Nederland%20(TMNL)

Pierce T, Wooldridge D (2014) The business of iOS app development. For iPhone, iPad and iPod touch, 3rd edn. Apress, New York

Rajput V (2013) Research on know your customer (KYC). Int J Sci Res Publ 3(7)

Ray P (2018) A survey on internet of things architectures. J King Saud Univ Comp Inf Sci 30(3): 291–319

Saia R et al (2019) Internet of Entities (IoE): A Blockchain-based Distributed Paradigm for Data Exchange between Wireless-based Devices. In: Proceedings of the 8th International Conference on Sensor Networks

Schirmer J (2020) Artificial intelligence and legal personality: introducing "Teilrechtsfähigkeit": a partial legal status made in Germany. In: Wischmeyer T, Rademacher T (eds) Regulating artificial intelligence. Springer, Cham

Serneels S (2023) Detecting wash trading for nonfungible tokens. Financ Res Lett 52:103374

Shaw D, Newholm T (2002) Voluntary simplicity and the ethics of consumption. Psychol Mark 19(2)

References

Sillaber C, Waltl B (2017) Life cycle of smart contracts in Blockchain ecosystems. Datenschutz und Datensicherheit 8

Sjöberg C (2020) The digital person-a new legal entity? On the role of law in an AI-based society. In: Corrales M (ed) Legal tech and the new sharing economy. Springer Nature, Singapore

Soltani R et al (2016) A new algorithm for money laundering detection based on structural similarity. UEMCON https://doi.org/10.1109/UEMCON.2016.7777919

Tzafestas S (2018) Ethics and law in the internet of things world. Smart Cities 1(1)

Van Eerten S, Van Heugten K (2018) Which digital innovations can enhance the combat of financial institutions to detect financial economic crime. Tijdschrift voor Compliance 2

Von Wachter V et al (2022) NFT wash trading: quantifying suspicious behaviour in NFT markets. Cryptography and security. Cornell University, Ithaca

Wachhaus T (2011) Anarchy as a model for network governance. Public Adm Rev 72(1):33–42

Wang Y et al (2019) Randomness invalidates criminal smart contracts. Inf Sci 477:291–301

Weber R (2009) Internet of things – need for a new legal environment? Comp Law Secur Rev 25(6): 522–527

Wen X et al (2023) NFTDisk: visual detection of wash trading in NFT Markets. Proceedings of the 2023 CHI Conference on Human Factors in Computing Systems

Wójtowicz A, Joachimiak K (2016) Model for adaptable context-based biometric authentication for mobile devices. Pers Ubiquit Comput 20:195–207

WRR (2019) Geld en Schuld. De publieke rol van banken. https://www.wrr.nl/publicaties/rapporten/2019/01/17/geld-en-schuld%2D%2D-de-publieke-rol-van-banken

Zhang L et al (2019) A game-theoretic method based on Q-learning to invalidate criminal smart contracts. Inf Sci 498:144–153

Ziemianin K (2021) Civil legal personality of artificial intelligence: Future or utopia? Internet Policy Rev 10(2)

Zouridis S, Leijtens V (2021) Bringing the law Back in: the law-government nexus in an era of network governance. Perspect Public Manag Governance 4(2)

Open Access This chapter is licensed under the terms of the Creative Commons Attribution 4.0 International License (http://creativecommons.org/licenses/by/4.0/), which permits use, sharing, adaptation, distribution and reproduction in any medium or format, as long as you give appropriate credit to the original author(s) and the source, provide a link to the Creative Commons license and indicate if changes were made.

The images or other third party material in this chapter are included in the chapter's Creative Commons license, unless indicated otherwise in a credit line to the material. If material is not included in the chapter's Creative Commons license and your intended use is not permitted by statutory regulation or exceeds the permitted use, you will need to obtain permission directly from the copyright holder.

Chapter 6
Currency (Layering)

6.1 Introduction

The previous chapter has examined the legal framework with regard to the placement phase of the Metaverse. The placement phase is however the first of the three general stages of MLFT. The second phase is that of layering. Layering is the term used to describe the process of concealing the origins of the funds. The main risk with regard to the Metaverse is a series of transactions with cryptocurrency in particular when these transactions are intended to hide their origins. The following paragraphs will discuss the so-called mixer and exchange services. Mixing services mix cryptocurrencies and redistribute them so that their origins cannot be traced to the original owner or exchanged the cryptocurrencies for other cryptocurrencies. The exchange services are services that exchange one cryptocurrency for the other. This service can be used either to get a different form of currency (the same way you could wish to exchange euros for pounds) or to create a layer between the dirty and clean tokens.

Another risk with the Metaverse is the different forms of currencies currently available. The legislation has to include all virtual currencies within its framework. If it does not include all forms of currency the risk is avoidance of supervision through different types of currency.

6.2 Cryptocurrencies

Cryptocurrencies and MLFT are linked to the point where they are nearly considered synonyms. The reason for the love between cryptocurrencies and MLFT is threefold. Cryptocurrencies can be transferred pseudonymously or anonymously. The transactions are furthermore not automatically screened and are instant. The anonymity was covered in the previous chapter in combination with monitoring possibilities

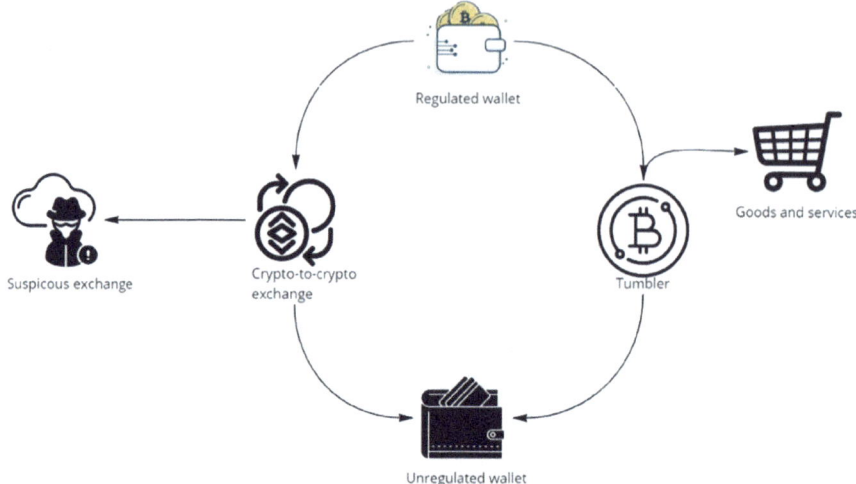

Fig. 6.1 Mixing services

through the wallet systems. The wallet system acts as a gatekeeper thus preventing anonymity at the door, right? Unfortunately, it is not that easy to prevent MLFT. There are possibilities to circumvent the gatekeepers, whether through smurfing, hacking or techniques yet to be invented. Once entered into the Metaverse economy the criminal will aim to layer the cryptocurrency through various transactions. It is at this stage that the AMLD5 exposes a gap in regulation with regard to cryptocurrencies. The AMLD5 aims to prevent MLFT via cryptocurrencies primarily through regulation of exchange services. Exchange services are defined as those exchanging virtual currencies for fiat currencies and vice versa.[1] The AMLD5 regulates the in- and output but fails to regulate the various crypto-to-crypto conversions. In particular, the AMLD5 regulates neither mixing services nor crypto-to-crypto exchanges.[2] Tumblers or mixing services act exactly as the name suggests. They mix cryptocurrencies for a fee to increase anonymity. This lack of regulation creates various risks in the approach to MLFT.

Figure 6.1 demonstrates some of the risks associated with crypto-to-crypto exchanges. The first wallet is regulated and sends a supervised transaction to the exchange or tumbler. The payout was made to an unregulated wallet. The unregulated wallet can then conduct various unsupervised transactions with a currency whose origins are nearly impossible to trace. The system that this book proposes in Chap. 5 seriously decreases the use of unregulated wallets. However, that system only works if there is no or little opportunity to exchange the illicit currency for licit currency. If the crypto-to-crypto exchange allows for the

---

[1] Article 1(1)c AMLD 5.
[2] Haffke, Fromberger and Zimmerman (2019), pp. 134–136.

6.2 Cryptocurrencies

unregulated wallets to exchange their cryptocurrency with payout to a regulated wallet, that would provide opportunities for MLFT. In addition, the exchanges and tumbler services can be used to directly pay for goods and services. Lastly, exchange services can be used to facilitate suspicious transactions. Through a peer-to-peer exchange goods and services can be sold which looks like a crypto-to-crypto exchange. I.e. a transaction whereby €500,- worth in cryptocurrency A is sold for a value of €100,- worth in cryptocurrency B is suspicious. It is more likely that the currency exchange is a cover for an illicit transaction worth around €400,-. These gaps in the regulation make it difficult to supervise suspicious activities. The additional layers provided by the mixers and exchanges furthermore increase the difficulty in tracing the origins of the coins. This example only used one exchange but the process could be repeated ten times over. The question is why these mixing and exchange practices are not simply banned.

Though mixers and exchanges of cryptocurrencies are generally associated with MLFT, its origins were not illegal. The idea came from the anarchist approach behind the development of cryptocurrencies of fully anonymous payments without government intervention. The bitcoin was considered by its designers as a protest against the commercial influence over legal currency.[3] The concept of privacy is considered political.[4] A debate that is furthermore fueled by the notion that data and personal information are a new class of assets.[5] Nevertheless whilst mixers and the like were perhaps not generated to launder money, these services are notorious for criminal activities.[6] Therefore providing a strong incentive to prohibit or at least regulate these services.

The difficulty with trying to regulate mixing services is the various alternatives that exist. Such as building an extra layer upon the blockchain that allows anonymization of the coin.[7] An approach to increase the traceability of transactions therefore has to include all possibilities of layering. The difficulty would be to include all options within the AMLD5. The legislator could try to provide a list prohibiting the different activities. The first obvious flaw within this suggestion is the list would be obsolete by the time it was published. Technology develops faster than the law. The second problem with this approach is that some of these technologies, such as crypto-to-crypto-platforms, promote trade. To avoid this problem the legislator could regulate the intention rather than the technology. The previous chapter discussed regulating digital entities through regulating the intention rather than the technology.[8] To fill the supervisory gap in the layering process the AMLD5 could include services to reduce traceability. The question is what then? Some suggest the

---

[3] Harvey and Branco-Illodo (2020), pp. 108.
[4] Ibid.
[5] World Economic Forum (2011).
[6] Wronka (2022), pp. 79–94; Haffke et al. (2019).
[7] Haffke et al. (2019).
[8] See Sect. 4.3.1. Digital Entity.

mixing services should be mandated to perform Know-Your-Customer duties.[9] Considering the concept of mixing services is to increase anonymity and reduce the traceability a KYC duty would either not be adhered to or the mixing would go bankrupt. It is therefore unlikely that the inclusion of such provisions would increase the effectiveness of the AMLD. In particular, because the FIUs are not without possibilities.

In 2018 the FIOD (the Dutch FIU) seized the website Bestmixer.io and took the website down.[10] The seizure was part of a coordinated investigation into money laundering activities. The investigation furthermore led to the arrest of two suspects.[11] The investigation was initiated based on a report provided by a cybersecurity company that had located the servers in the Netherlands and Luxembourg.[12] The resulting seizure had been conducted by the FIOD and the public prosecutor. It is not officially stated but the involvement of the public prosecution's office implies the foundation for this operation to be Dutch criminal law, not AML legislation. From a supervisory perspective, the lack of legislation on mixers does not have to be a cause for worry. If the criminal code of a country is up to date on aiding and abetting MLFT. It then moves the responsibility to the national FIU as part of a criminal investigation rather than a supervisory one. Nevertheless, this solution is a bit odd. It assumes that mixers are not per se illegal, as mixing is not per definition illegal. If, however, a mixer attracts too much attention from money launderers it will be shut down. Whether a mixer attracts money launderers is fairly arbitrary as they are not required KYC duties. Charging a mixer service with KYC duties is somewhat contrary to its intentions, it would however reduce the arbitrariness. The second danger with regard to layering is that of the crypto-to-crypto exchange services.

The crypto-to-crypto exchange services are more difficult to regulate. Technically the exchange services can be regulated similarly to the fiat-to-crypto exchange services. The difficulty with this approach is that it works only with centralized crypto exchanges. Centralized exchanges work with a central party buying and selling cryptocurrency. The centralized party can be placed within the AML framework and charged with due diligence duties. In addition to centralized exchanges, there are decentralized crypto exchanges or DEX. These exchanges can operate by facilitating a peer-to-peer exchange platform or from purchase and sale to a liquidity pool. The traders do not provide access to their private keys and do not need an account but simply connect their wallet to the DEX. To regulate a DEX is therefore

---

[9] Europol. Multi-million euro cryptocurrency laundering service Bestmixer.io taken down https://www.europol.europa.eu/media-press/newsroom/news/multi-million-euro-cryptocurrency-laundering-service-bestmixerio-taken-down.

[10] FIOD (2019) FIOD en OM halen witwasmachine voor cryptovaluta offline. https://www.fiod.nl/fiod-en-om-halen-witwasmachine-voor-cryptovaluta-offline/.

[11] FIOD (2020) Twee aanhoudingen in twee onderzoeken naar witwassen met cryptovaluta. https://www.fiod.nl/twee-aanhoudingen-in-twee-onderzoeken-naar-witwassen-met-cryptovaluta/.

[12] FIOD (2019) FIOD en OM halen witwasmachine voor cryptovaluta offline. https://www.fiod.nl/fiod-en-om-halen-witwasmachine-voor-cryptovaluta-offline/.

6.2 Cryptocurrencies

more difficult because traders can automatically connect to the platform without the need for the operator to verify their information.

The primary method for a DEX to function on is that of the automated marker method (AMM) which functions on a liquidity pool. The liquidity pool is a pool of various crypto coins available within the DEX. The DEX then functions upon an algorithm and smart contract that allows a user to buy and sell tokens against those in the store. The more tokens of a kind that are held in the pool, the lower the value. If tokens are being bought the price rises which incentivizes other traders to supply that coin to the pool. This type of transaction means that it will be difficult for two parties to conduct a suspicious transaction. As the transactions are not peer-to-peer but rather peer-to-pool. The only option is that of transferring between wallets through a DEX (wallet A buys and wallet B receives payout). A simple solution would be to legally limit such transactions to a single wallet. The result would be that wallet A buys and wallet A receives a payout. This would not decrease the tracing difficulty but because the transaction remains within the same wallet. Because the currencies remain within the wallet, the wallet's algorithm would become suspicious if a high frequency of conversions takes place. The second category of DEXs are those that run via the order book method.

The order book method is a type of facilitator whereby one party offers a sale or purchase of coins against a price and another accepts. The DEX thus facilitates a peer-to-peer platform. This type of platform can facilitate a suspicious transaction. It is, however, a risky form of transacting as anyone can accept the terms offered by one of the parties. The order book matches the two parties for the transaction. Furthermore, the wallets directly transact with each other. Therefore the connection between the two parties' wallets is present. A suspicious swap can therefore be linked to both parties. The order book can be equipped with an algorithm that detects suspicious transactions. Nevertheless, suspicious transaction detection is unfunctional unless it can be reported. Some argue therefore that DEXs should be included in the legal framework as an obliged entity with KYC duties.[13] This would mean that the DEX would have to redesign its platform and only allow users with an account access. Increasing the scope of the AMLD to include DEXs is not necessarily a bad approach. Including the DEX under the scope of the AMLD would have to be responsive to the level of risk. Different levels of KYC should therefore be applicable.

A DEX that operates through an automated marker method carries lower MLFT risk. In particular, if that wallet is supervised and if the transaction is only between one wallet and the liquidity pool. The value remains within the same wallet which monitors the transactions. A DEX that facilitates the exchange of coins through AMM with unsupervised wallets, should have higher KYC duties. A DEX that facilitates peer-to-peer transactions and two wallets in a single transaction carries the highest MLFT risks. Such a DEX could thus be mandated to always conduct a more thorough KYC duty. This means that a potential exchange first requires those

---

[13] Haffke et al. (2019), p. 92.

wanting to buy or sell to create a verified account with the DEX. This type of KYC might, however, generate some resistance.

Cryptocurrencies were invented to reduce government supervision and traceability. It is therefore not an unreasonable expectation to consider that a significant amount of users will try to avoid these regulations. Either for malicious activities or under the motto "I have nothing to hide but neither does a third party need to track my behaviour". To mitigate this behavior an alternative route can be considered.

The alternative considers the wallets as part of the Internet of Things. The wallets contain all the necessary information of their users. These wallets when transacting are connected to a device whether through a USB port or as software. These devices within the IoT are referred to as the perception layer. This layer needs to connect to the internet through a router or other port. This device is sometimes referred to as the "fog layer". The fog can be equipped with a verifier that verifies the information of the user (location etc.).[14] The information is stored on the fog layer which encrypts the information and stores it on a blockchain only accessible to law enforcement.[15] When an investigation requires the decryption the fog layer will verify the request of the law enforcer. Once verified, it will allow it to run forensic applications present on the fog layer.[16] This data is then stored on a consortium blockchain only accessible to law enforcers.[17] Thus demonstrating greater transparency for suspects to determine the chain of evidence. Devices can be traded anonymously unless they are under investigation. Though such a system is a middle ground between anonymous and public transactions it requires a few changes. A verification system would be required to ensure that a forensic application can only be triggered in compliance with a court order (or other legal requirement). Secondly, the encrypted information should not be shared with jurisdictions that have little government limitations. In the EU most national courts would not provide an order for forensic investigation unless there is a serious suspicion. This legal protection is not present in all countries and would be very useful to autocratic regimes wishing to spy on their population. Within the EU it would be recommended to operate a consortium blockchain only for the EU Member States. The judicial oversight could be shared between the national courts and in major investigations the new to-be-founded EU MLFT agent. The latter could be overseen by the Court of Justice of the European Union (CJEU). This approach would be effective but difficult. Unlike national Member States, the EU does not have a criminal code of sorts. The EU has a Charter of Fundamental Rights but no rules on criminal procedures. The lack of such rules would create confusion for all parties involved. Technically such rules could be written but at the EU level, it will be difficult to reach a consensus. It would however decrease the amount of user data that is available to third parties.

---

[14] Kumar et al. (2021), p. 17.
[15] Ibid.
[16] Ibid, p. 18.
[17] Ibid.

The current approach to data and privacy protection is that all information on the customer is processed by the entity that is obliged to control suspicious activities. The bank that monitors its client's bank account has access to all transactions and the full customer profile. The bank is obliged not to use that information without the customer's consent, other than monitoring for suspicious activity.[18] Nevertheless, this requires the customer to trust the bank not to use that information, other than for monitoring purposes. The bank furthermore may not legally break that trust. It is, however, exactly that trust in banks (and other intermediaries) that many of the cryptocurrency users lack. The proposed system allows encrypted communication between various wallets, whereby data is only shared when wanted. The financial investigative units can only access the data through a court order. This type of approach is a more bottom-up form of data ownership. The data is owned by the person where it is generated, rather than where the law places the ownership. The approach is legally more sensible because the de facto control of data is present within the individual.[19] The approach is closer aligned with the original anarchist views behind cryptocurrency development. To generate this type of system data protection should be built into the wallets.[20]

6.3 Centralized Currency Issuers

The more famous cryptocurrencies such as bitcoin are decentralized and operate through a blockchain. To transfer such assets the security keys are necessary. There are, however, centralized currencies as well. These types of currencies would not work through a cryptographic key perse. Typically closed systems and one-directional currencies work through central administration. But also the L$ used in the game Second Life is a centralized currency. Furthermore whilst the attempts of Meta to introduce its own currency remain unsuccessful, it is not unlikely another company will introduce a centralized currency. In particular, within the Metaverse the providers of successful virtual realities can introduce their own currency. These currencies have the potential to be used for MLFT purposes either through (black market) conversion or by a wide-level redemption. These systems operate without cryptographic keys but on ledgers and with customer accounts. A literal interpretation would therefore exclude the wallet and thereby such currencies from supervision. The question is, if a purposive interpretation is used, would such currencies fall under the definition of virtual currency? The AMDL5 defines virtual currencies as:

---

[18] See article 6 of Regulation (EU) 2016/679 (General Data Protection Regulation) OJ L 119, 04.05.2016.
[19] Janeček (2018), p. 1045.
[20] Tyagi et al. (2014), pp. 29–35.

> "virtual currencies" means a digital representation of value that is not issued or guaranteed by a central bank or a public authority, is not necessarily attached to a legally established currency and does not possess a legal status of currency or money, but is accepted by natural or legal persons as a means of exchange and which can be transferred, stored and traded electronically.[21]

This definition is phrased quite broadly and can include many types of currencies. Whilst phrased quite broadly there are several criteria before something can be considered a virtual currency. These criteria are: electronically represented value, not provided by a central bank or government, without the legal status of a currency but accepted as a means of trade and electronically transferable. Within the Metaverse there are likely several forms of currency. It is questionable whether all of these fall within the definition of virtual currency. In particular, whether currencies other than cryptocurrencies are covered by this legislation.

The previous chapter covered wallet providers and discussed the legal differentiation through safeguarding a cryptographic key. Whilst the section concluded that the cryptographic key is not the crucial criterion, it demonstrates another issue. The legislator intended to regulate cryptocurrencies. These currencies are generally provided through a decentralized ledger system. There is no centralized ledger that monitors the transactions as an account-based bank would. So let's imagine a centralized currency is introduced successfully. The law currently regulates the exchange services and the wallets. The issuer of the centralized currency could provide the wallets and thus monitor the transactions. The currency can however also potentially be held by other wallets than those of the issuer. The current legal framework is circled around exchange and wallet services. It excludes the role of the issuer. Not regulating the issuer risks various issues. A blockchain trail depends on its level of encryption but ledgers can be easily followed. Whilst banks are under supervision and have to comply with EU legislation, the same does not naturally follow for centralized currency issuers. The issuers might not be located in the EU and even when they are they are not regulated. To regulate the issuers the same as wallet providers carries some argument. The issuer would have full access to the transaction ledger and thus be able to supervise transactions. However, when compared to fiat currency there is no such obligation for the central banks as issuers of currency. The task of a central bank with regard to MLFT is to provide guidance and supervise supervising entities.[22] It therefore raises the question of whether issuers should be given any monitoring duties. Or whether these issuers should be regulated as if they were central banks and therefore be the supervisors of the wallet. This approach may seem logical as issuers are the private law equivalent of central banks. Nevertheless, the question is then who supervises the issuers? Thus perhaps

---

[21] Article 1(2) sub d, Directive (EU) 2018/843 of the European Parliament and of the Council of 30 May 2018 amending Directive (EU) 2015/849 on the prevention of the use of the financial system for the purposes of money laundering or terrorist financing, and amending Directives 2009/138/EC and 2013/36/EU (Text with EEA relevance).

[22] Demetriades and Vassileva (2020), pp. 509–533.

indicating the issuers should be regulated as if they were mere wallet providers. To regulate issuers as wallets would be a difficult task.

The difference between centralized currencies and cryptocurrency is the money trail. The MLFT risk of a blockchain is evaluated through the three questions. Who is in charge of the encryption, can it be decrypted and what is the cost for a third party to decrypt the network?[23] These questions assess the anonymity of a blockchain. The issuer has direct access to the paper trail through its ledger. It would therefore be prudent to regulate the circumstances under which an issuer has to hand over its ledger to the investigating authorities. However, this raises the question of what responsibilities these issuers have towards the wallets. Defining the role of issuers of private centralized currency is therefore a difficult task. It would be this author's suggestion to create a new level of responsibility for issuers. One is that they are responsible for monitoring their centralized ledger and any wallet providers. Nevertheless, they should do so under close supervision of the national authorities. Considering the variety of virtual currencies the monitoring duties of the issuer could even be adjusted to fit the currency's structure. Though this would shape the responsibilities of the issuers of centralized currency it does not provide a comprehensive framework towards all virtual currencies available.

6.4 Legal Tender

The currencies in the Metaverse will all be digital and electronically transferable. However more problematic is whether all of these means of payment possess value and are not provided by a central bank. There are two developments with regard to legal tender and the virtual environment which need to be considered. The first is that of Central Bank Digital Currency (CBDC), a type of electronic currency that is provided by a central bank. The ECB is currently researching the possibility of introducing a digital euro.[24] The CBDC would be provided by a central bank and therefore not considered a virtual currency. Thus excluding a digital euro from supervision under the AML framework.

6.4.1 The Digital Euro

There are various options on how to design a digital euro. The ECB will first have to decide between a token or an account-based digital euro. The second decision is whether the digital euro will operate through a one-tier or two-tier system. The first is one whereby the consumer is given access to the digital euro directly through the

---

[23] Papadopoulos (2015), p. 157; (see Sect. 4.3.1).
[24] European Central Bank (2020).

central bank. The two-tier system will involve consumer access through commercial banks or other financial actors. The one-tier system would be the more dangerous choice as it would require the central banks as monitoring entities. Currently in jurisdictions such as the Netherlands the central bank also supervises commercial banks on the compliance of the AMLD. Effectively the supervisor would supervise himself. It is, however, unlikely that the ECB would be able to lawfully introduce a one-tier digital euro.[25] The more likely choice is that the ECB will introduce a two-tier digital euro. This design option has also been put forward by the EU Commission in its legislative proposal concerning the digital euro.[26] The second choice is whether the ECB will introduce the digital euro token or account-based. A token or bearer-based digital euro would allow the owner of the digital euro to transfer the token through wallet options, not unlike cash or the current cryptocurrency.[27] An account-based digital euro would resemble the current bank accounts.

Account-based digital euros rely on the identification of customers. They are therefore considered less risky.[28] Concerning supervision, the token-based option is arguably the most risky, in particular if the transactions are not recorded on a central ledger.[29] A token, like cash, could be traded without the need for identification. Similar to cash, tokens run the risk of being traded without verification.[30] This risk is present but does not seem like a substantial danger when considering the digital euro. In particular, the ECB writes that if a token-based design is chosen for the digital euro it would be traded through a device capable of identifying the holder.[31] It is thus unlikely that a token-based digital euro would be traded in full anonymity. This likelihood is further decreased because the current proposal is to incorporate the digital euro with the EU digital identity wallet.[32] The current proposal of the Commission considers a two-tier system whereby the public has access to the digital euro.[33] Because the public has access to the digital euro it can be used for MLFT purposes.[34] The Commission proposes that the AML requirements remain the responsibility of the intermediaries.[35] It therefore creates a similar system to that

---

[25] Mooij (2022).

[26] Proposal for a REGULATION OF THE EUROPEAN PARLIAMENT AND OF THE COUNCIL on the establishment of the digital euro COM/2023/369.

[27] The report on the digital euro does however state a token based euro does not have to be based upon a blockchain.

[28] Dupuis and Gleason (2022), p. 174.

[29] Ibid, p. 180.

[30] Ibid, p. 174.

[31] European Central Bank (2020) and European Central Bank & Bank of Japan (2020).

[32] Proposal for a REGULATION OF THE EUROPEAN PARLIAMENT AND OF THE COUNCIL on the establishment of the digital euro COM/2023/369., article 25.

[33] Ibid.

[34] Dupuis et al. (2022), pp. 174–175.

[35] Proposal for a REGULATION OF THE EUROPEAN PARLIAMENT AND OF THE COUNCIL on the establishment of the digital euro COM/2023/369.

6.4 Legal Tender

of the bank accounts. The main difference between regular bank accounts and CBDC is that of offline payments. The digital euro will incorporate the possibility to pay offline. This type of payment, however, will require the transacting parties to be in close physical proximity to each other.[36] The requirement for close physical proximity makes this possibility low risk with regard to the Metaverse.

Whilst there is still some uncertainty concerning the digital euro, it is not likely to become an AML loophole. The ECB report does not provide conclusions on the AMLD framework.[37] The report, however, does consider the risks of MLFT and considers these should be addressed appropriately. Considering that the ECB is taking these risks on board it is unlikely the digital euro will not be supervised. The current legislative proposal furthermore addresses MLFT and brings the digital euro under the supervisory framework through commercial banks. The introduction of CBDC is therefore not the biggest threat facing the Metaverse as it is likely to be incorporated into the heavily regulated banking sector.

The digital euro is, however, not the only digital central bank currency. More countries have introduced or are investigating the introduction of central bank digital currencies. The BIS found that in 2022 93% of central banks are working on some form of central bank digital currency.[38] One of such countries to have introduced a central bank digital currency is Nigeria. The eNaira is, unlike the proposed digital euro, based upon a blockchain. The currency can be accessed through a virtual wallet called the "eNaira Speed App".[39] This virtual wallet makes use of various remote identifyers. Users without bank account must upload their passport in order to use the app.[40] Nevertheless there are concerns with regard to MLFT. The compliance with MLFT regulations in Nigeria is considered lacking.[41] The eNaira is build upon a private blockchain called Hyperledger Fabric.[42] The private blockchain is limited to communicate with the eNaira wallets.[43] This means that using the eNaira wallet in the Metaverse comes with significant limitations. A person from Nigeria living in the EU can access and use an eNaira wallet in the EU. In theory this transfers MLFT risks to the EU. At present the adoption of the eNaira however is limited, thus limiting MLFT risks for the EU. In the future however it is likely that the central bank digital currencies can interoperate with each other. This could highly increase the risk of MLFT as some CBDCs will be better supervised than others.

There are several possibilities to reduce the risk of MLFT via foreign currencies. One option is to ensure that virtual wallets can only host CBDCs of the jurisdiction in which they are located. Before entering the virtual wallet all foreign currencies

---

[36] Ibid.
[37] European Central Bank (2020), p. 4.
[38] Kosse and Mattei (2023), p. 1.
[39] Esoimeme (2021), p. 10.
[40] Ibid.
[41] Ibid, pp. 13–14.
[42] Rawat (2023).
[43] Ree (2021).

will be first converted. The only currency within the EU registered wallets would then be digital euros. The wallet should register the conversions as foreign transactions. If such transactions become suspicious the same legal framework applies as described in Sect. 5.6.

Another likely problem to be is that countries will recognize cryptocurrency as a legal tender. Therefore potentially excluding these currencies from the definition of virtual currencies.

6.4.2 Cryptocurrencies As Legal Tender

Globally speaking there are many regions where people are either un or underbanked. The reasons vary from no physical access to banks or the costs involved with a bank account.[44] Digital currencies can provide financial inclusion when people have internet access. Financial inclusion has its benefits to the extent that countries consider recognizing them as legal tender. Recognizing a cryptocurrency as legal tender would conflict with the virtual currency criterion of *"value that is not issued or guaranteed by a central bank"* and *"does not possess a legal status of currency or money"*. If a virtual currency does not qualify as virtual currency and can be accessed without the need for a bank, this risks exclusion from the supervisory framework. The first country to have recognized a cryptocurrency as a legal tender is El Salvador. The recognition is widely believed as a marketing stunt, as few people have access to the internet. Nevertheless, there are some economic reasons as to why El Salvador introduced Bitcoin as a legal tender.

It is estimated that roughly 24% of El Salvador's GDP consists of remittances sent home from abroad.[45] Sending remittances through traditional channels is a very costly and lengthy process. Cryptocurrencies can be sent internationally at much greater speed against much lower costs.[46] The economy of El Salvador would therefore stand to benefit from introducing Bitcoin as a legal tender. The volatility of the cryptocurrency is of little consequence to the costs of remittance if the cryptocurrency can be exchanged for fiat currency immediately. Remittance workers have therefore discovered the benefits of using cryptocurrency.[47] The recognition of Bitcoin as legal tender in El Salvador, however, has cost the country millions and El Salvador faces pressure to abolish its use.[48] This was largely due to the poor implementation of the wallet system. Furthermore, many people in El Salvador do

---

[44] Traynor et al. (2017), p. 1.
[45] Kshetri (2022a), p. 85.
[46] Naderi (2021).
[47] Flore (2018), pp. 17–25.
[48] Linthicum (2022).

not understand Bitcoin technology.[49] Using Bitcoin furthermore makes it difficult for people to save as the currency is so volatile.[50]

Another reason to introduce cryptocurrency as legal tender is to achieve monetary sovereignty. The Central African Republic (CAR) did not have its own currency. Instead, it used a currency introduced by the French which was pegged to the Euro. This has as disadvantage that the country cannot conduct its own monetary policy.[51] The introduction of a cryptocurrency has the advantage that it can cheaply introduce a monetary system. It does not require the setting up of a printing press or to back up the money with a stable value such as gold. It is however difficult to introduce such a system as it requires widespread internet and electricity access in combination with a high level of digital skills. Additionally, whilst Furthermore in such cases it is more likely that a country would turn to the earlier discussed CBDC, rather than cryptocurrencies. Currently, the danger that cryptocurrencies will be widely recognized as legal tender is therefore limited. There are however instances where virtual currencies would be preferential to the legal tender.

In Venezuela, hyperinflation severely damaged the economy and there was little trust in the national currency. The Venezuelans en masse started to play a virtual game called Old School Rune Scape (ORS). Within this game, they would collect ORS gold through farming and beating warriors. They would then sell the gold to other players worldwide for fiat currency, in particular for US Dollars.[52] These dollars were exchanged into the Venezuelan Bolivar when needed for groceries. Thus allowing the Venezuelan to generate a stable income of roughly $100 per month. An income far above the minimum wage which was about $5 a month.[53] Earning and saving their income in gaming currency which could be converted to dollars furthermore allowed them to avoid the high inflation. The inflation rate in 2018 in Venezuela was estimated to be between 100.000 and 150.000%.[54] The US Dollars and ORS gold were more stable in value and thus preferred to the national currency. As a result over 50% of transactions in Venezuela were conducted in dollars.[55] The adaptation whether officially or unofficially, of a foreign currency as a national currency brings risks.

The first risk is that the currency is physically not available. Physical bills are often scarce and the technology to verify the authenticity of the currency is often not available. Zimbabwe experienced this issue during its time of hyperinflation whereby worn and torn dollar bills were used.[56] Adapting a virtual currency

---

[49] Kshetri (2022a, p. 87.
[50] Ibid.
[51] Kshetri (2022b).
[52] Ombler (2020) and Maat (2020).
[53] Ombler (2020).
[54] WorldData (2022). Development of inflation rates in Venezuela. https://www.worlddata.info/america/venezuela/inflation-rates.php.
[55] Zerpa Fabioloa (2019).
[56] Chingono Nyasha (2021).

would solve the scarcity of bills. The ORS gold was not used by shopkeepers in Venezuela, as it would require both parties to log in to their Rune Scape account to conduct payment for a transaction. The Metaverse, however, would be able to facilitate the use of such virtual currencies for day-to-day transactions. The shopkeeper and customer would need to have a virtual account with a wallet. The customer upon buying groceries would only need to enter the virtual reality through his or her phone and pay the shopkeeper. Technically such transactions can already be facilitated through wallet services. The Metaverse, however, will have another advantage. Hyperinflation is often associated with the scarcity of goods.[57] In Venezuela, people had to wait in line for basic supplies, and often waiting was in vain.[58] Shops furthermore risked looting, as people were desperate for supplies.[59] The Metaverse can facilitate online grocery shopping thus preventing the need for long lineups. It furthermore can increase safety as shopkeepers do not need to provide physical locations but can deliver. Thus limiting the possibility of robberies and looting of their shops. This type of infrastructure in combination with virtual currency earned online can mitigate some of the effects of hyperinflation. In the case of Venezuela, people could transfer their ORS gold to virtual currency and use it to buy basic goods in the local Metaverse shops. The Metaverse shop owners can then deliver the goods during the day, without providing a physical location of their shop. In such a scenario a virtual currency will become the de facto legal tender. This could materialize in different ways. The first is whereby a foreign fiat currency, a (combination of) cryptocurrencies or a virtual currency is recognized as legal tender. Whilst a fiat currency will require some form of bank, virtual currencies do not. Thus raising the question of whether these will be supervised.

When comparing cryptocurrencies with CBDC there is a clear difference between virtual currencies managed by a central bank or government and those that are not. The criterion of legal tender should be read in conjunction with the criterion of issued or guaranteed by a government or central bank. The EBA further considers that a virtual currency is not necessarily pegged to a fiat currency or redeemable at par by the issuer.[60] The recognition of virtual currencies by governments does not mean the government will consider them redeemable at par or even is the issuer. Recognition would therefore not necessarily interfere with the possibility of supervision. This legal tender criterion, however, is also approached from the functionality of money perspective. Money serves three functions, means of trade, store of value and unit of account. It is then argued that virtual currency does not fulfil the criteria of money because they are not accepted by the government. Thus they cannot be used as a unit of trade.[61] From this perspective, the cryptocurrency would be considered legal tender equal to that of 'normal' fiat currency. If the cryptocurrency

---

[57] Arisson (2018); Kalecki (1962), pp. 275–281.
[58] Charner and Newton (2016).
[59] Ulmer and Chinea (2015).
[60] European Banking Authority (2014), p. 11.
[61] Dabrowski and Janikowski (2018), p. 7.

6.4 Legal Tender

is recognized as legal tender and de facto used as legal tender this fulfills the criteria for money. The definition of money then relies on whether it is considered and used as legal tender. Whilst technically easy to define, the scenario of Venezuela and El Salvador proves the opposite. Bitcoin might be recognized in El Salvador as a legal tender but is not used as such. In situations such as those with Venezuela, virtual currency can be used as legal tender but not recognized as such. Whilst most of these scenarios play out outside the EU, it is relevant to the European framework. When a cryptocurrency is considered as legal tender this renders it outside the definition of 'virtual currency' under AMLD5. Thus raising the question of the monitoring duties of the wallets storing the currency.

As stated above there are two approaches to interpretation of legal tender. The first is reading the criterion in combination with issued and/or guaranteed by a government or central bank. The second is according to the functionality of money. If the first approach is used in situations such as those described above would not change the definition of i.e. Bitcoin as a virtual currency. The status of legal tender does not change that it is not issued nor guaranteed by a central bank or government. If the second approach, that of the functionality of money, is used it provides two difficulties. The first is when to consider a currency to be accepted as legal tender. When the government recognizes the currency or when it is generally accepted? Secondly, if such currencies are recognized and used as legal tender would they fall under AMLD supervision? The AMLD framework covers virtual currencies and various institutes of payment services such as banks. These institutions function as the 'gatekeepers' to the financial system.[62] The financial institutions monitor the fiat currency transactions. The legal tender cryptocurrencies would not need such an institution to be transferred. Nor would they fall under the definition of virtual currency.

To avoid this loophole the most straightforward approach is to consider a currency not a virtual currency only when it is both legal tender and issued by a central bank or government. The central bank or government issuing the currency would be responsible for bringing it under AML supervision. A country with little supervision would qualify as risky and those with high supervision as less risky. Thus creating a situation that is not very different from the current approach to transactions abroad. Whereby the EU has drafted a list of high-risk countries. Under the current circumstances, however, transferring/holding money in a foreign currency requires either cash exchange or an account abroad. The legal exchange of cash is monitored and going abroad to open an account is difficult and the transfer of funds from the EU to the account is monitored by banks. Under the current AMLD5, the exchange of fiat currency to virtual currency is regulated. The transfer of a legal tender virtual currency to a non-official virtual currency would fall under supervision. Buying virtual legal tender with fiat currency would be likely considered a currency exchange institution. Once in the wallet, the wallet would need either to be classified as a payment institution or remain part of the AMLD as a wallet provider.

---

[62] Dorant and Verbruggen (2020), p. 29.

Both would have monitoring duties but clarity is recommendable, as payment institutions require a permit and wallets only require registration. Whilst the definition of payment institutions is aimed at the EER, there is nothing in the Directive on payment services to prevent something from classifying as a payment service when the transactions occur in non-EER currencies.[63] The regulatory danger is therefore not so much in the lack of regulation but rather in the unclarity. To avoid any confusion it would be wise for the EU legislator to consider a statement on this topic. In particular, it would be this book's recommendation to keep all wallets under the same supervisory definition, without differentiation between virtual currency that is recognized and that is not recognized as legal tender. Thus avoiding any potential unclarity and loopholes.

Legal tender deserves attention from the EU legislator. Though the risks are not as high from legal tender in comparison with non-custodian wallets, there is some unclarity in the framework. The risks of the Metaverse, however, will extend beyond the currencies considered legal tender. The second criterion that may create exclusion is that of the 'accepted as means of exchange'. In particular when the currency has a (theoretically) limited redemption rate.

6.5 Conclusion and Recommendations

The layering of funds through the Metaverse is a real risk. It seems that the current legal framework is not yet adapted to respond to the new technologies available. The law focuses on the entrance of the funds to the Metaverse through the exchange providers. The law does regulate wallets which were discussed in the previous chapter, but does little to regulate the possibilities of layering through other means. It would therefore be recommended to increase the scope of the AMLD to include layering technologies such as mixing services and crypto-to-crypto exchanges. Though it may result in criminal mixing and exchange services, regulating the services makes it easier for law enforcement to act against criminal sites.

Additionally, there are various types of currency that are or are likely to exist in the Metaverse. Some of these currencies such as CBDCs are likely to be designed with an MLFT framework. These CBDCs carry lower risks than for example the centralized virtual currencies. Additionally, it is not clear what legal framework applies to virtual currencies when recognized as legal tender. It would be recommendable for these issues to be crystalized before the Metaverse increases its user base.

---

[63] Directive (EU) 2015/2366 of the European Parliament and of the Council of 25 November 2015 on payment services in the internal market, amending Directives 2002/65/EC, 2009/110/EC and 2013/36/EU and Regulation (EU) No 1093/2010, and repealing Directive 2007/64/EC (Text with EEA relevance).

These suggestions would increase the effectiveness of the supervision of the layering phase. The layering phase however is only the second phase out of three. The next chapter will therefore continue with the third phase of MLFT, namely that of the integration.

References

Arisson M (2018) Inflation and hyperinflation. In: Investing in the age of democracy. Palgrave Macmillan, Cham
Charner F, Newton P (2016) Venezuelans in long lines: 'We need food and medicine'. CNN 03 May
Chingono Nyasha (2021) Dirty dollars: how tattered US notes became the latest street hustle in Zimbabwe. The Guardian, 17 November
Dabrowski M, Janikowski (2018) Virtual currencies and central banks monetary policy: challenges ahead. Monetary Dialogue July
Demetriades P, Vassileva R (2020) Money laundering and central Bank governance in the European Union. J Int Econ Law 23(2):1–25
Dorant J, Verbruggen A (2020) Recente ontwikkelingen witwassen. TBS&H 1
Dupuis D, Gleason K (2022) Money laundering in a CBDC world: a game of cats and mice. J Financ Crime 29(1)
Dupuis D, Gleason K, Wang Z (2022) Money laundering in a CBDC world: a game of cats and mice. J Financ Crime
Esoimeme E (2021) A critical analysis of the effects of the Central Bank of Nigeria's digital currency named ENaira on financial inclusion and AML/CFT Measures. SSRN. https://doi.org/10.2139/ssrn.3921396
European Banking Authority (2014) Opinion on 'Virtual Currencies'. Frankfurt. https://www.eba.europa.eu/sites/default/documents/files/documents/10180/657547/81409b94-4222-45d7-ba3b-7deb5863ab57/EBA-Op-2014-08%20Opinion%20on%20Virtual%20Currencies.pdf?retry=1
European Central Bank (2020) Report on a digital euro. Frankfurt. Available at: https://www.ecb.europa.eu/pub/pdf/other/Report_on_a_digital_euro~4d7268b458.en.pdf
European Central Bank & Bank of Japan (2020) Balancing confidentiality and auditability in a distributed ledger environment. https://www.ecb.europa.eu/paym/intro/publications/pdf/ecb.miptopical200212.en.pdf
Flore M (2018) How blockchain-based technology is disrupting migrants' remittances: a preliminary assessment. JRC Science for policy report
Haffke L, Fromberger M, Zimmerman P (2019) Cryptocurrencies and anti-money laundering: the shortcomongs of the fifth AML directive (EU) and how to address them. J Bank Regul 21:125–138
Harvey J, Branco-Illodo I (2020) Why cryptocurrencies want privacy: a review of political motivations and branding Exressid in "privacy coin". J Polit Market 19
Janeček V (2018) Ownership of personal data in the internet of things. Comp Law Security Rev 34(5):1039–1052
Kalecki M (1962) A model of hyperinflation. Manch School 30(3)
Kosse A, Mattei I (2023) BIS Papers No 136 Making headway – Results of the 2022 BIS survey on central bank digital currencies and crypto. BIS report from Monetary and Economic Department. https://www.bis.org/publ/bppdf/bispap136.pdf
Kshetri N (2022a) El Salvador's Bitcoin Gamble. Computing's Economics
Kshetri N (2022b) Bitcoin's adoption as legal tender: a tale of two developing countries. IT Economics

Kumar G et al (2021) Internet-of-forensic (IoF): a blockchain based digital forensics framework for IoT applications. Futur Gener Comput Syst 120:13–25

Linthicum K (2022) El Salvador's president buys bitcoins 'naked,' he boasts. His experiment is costing his nation millions. LA Times 23 February

Maat A (2020) Why Venezuelans are ganging up on Old School Runescape to combat the effects of an economic crisis. Masters of Media, 27 September

Mooij A (2022) A digital euro for everyone: can the European system of central banks introduce general purpose CBDC as part of its economic mandate? J Bank Regul 24:89–10

Naderi N (2021) Utilizing blockchian technology in international remittances for poverty reduction and inclusive growth. Springer, Cham

Ombler M (2020) How RuneScape is helping Venezuelans survive. For years, Venezuelan players have been making a living by playing RuneScape. Polygon, 27 May

Papadopoulos G (2015) Blockchain and digital payments: an institutionalist analysis of cryptocurrencies. In: Chuen D (ed) Handbook of digital currency: bitcoin, innovation, financial instruments, and big data. Elsevier Science & Technology, Amsterdam

Rawat P (2023) Nigeria's eNaira CBDC: what went wrong? Cornell SC Johnson College of Business

Ree J (2021) Five observations on Nigeria's Central Bank digital currency, IMF African Department 16 November

Traynor P, Butler K, Bowers J (2017) FinTechSec: addressing the security challenges of digital financial services. Systems attacks and defences September/October

Tyagi S, Darwish A, Khan M (2014) Managing computing infrastructure for IoT data. Adv Internet Things 4:29–35

Ulmer A, Chinea E (2015) Robbers target food delivery trucks in shortage-hit Venezuela. Reuters, 23 January

World Economic Forum (2011) Personal data: the emergence of a new asset class. https://www3.weforum.org/docs/WEF_ITTC_PersonalDataNewAsset_Report_2011.pdf

Wronka C (2022) Money laundering through cryptocurrencies – analysis of the phenomenon and appropriate prevention measures. J Money Laund Control 25(1)

Zerpa Fabioloa (2019) Venezuela is now more than 50% dollarized, study finds. Bloomberg, 11 May

Open Access This chapter is licensed under the terms of the Creative Commons Attribution 4.0 International License (http://creativecommons.org/licenses/by/4.0/), which permits use, sharing, adaptation, distribution and reproduction in any medium or format, as long as you give appropriate credit to the original author(s) and the source, provide a link to the Creative Commons license and indicate if changes were made.

The images or other third party material in this chapter are included in the chapter's Creative Commons license, unless indicated otherwise in a credit line to the material. If material is not included in the chapter's Creative Commons license and your intended use is not permitted by statutory regulation or exceeds the permitted use, you will need to obtain permission directly from the copyright holder.

Chapter 7
Integration into the Legal Economy

7.1 Introduction

The third phase of MLFT is that of integration into the legal economy. The legal economy is where the funds are converted into the assets that can be enjoyed. The enjoyment entails both legal fiat currency and luxury items as "reward" for criminal activities. The various convictions of money launderers demonstrate the different rewards criminals provide themselves with. These type of goods include investing in real estate, luxury cars and holidays.[1] These type of luxury items are popular rewards that need to be integrated into the economy. The advantage for legislators is that owning a luxury car is noticeable. A car must be purchased to someone's name as must its insurance the same applies to real estate. In most developed jurisdictions the tax authorities will raise questions if someone on a low income manages to buy an expensive car or house. Money launderers therefore need to find a way to integrate their dirty funds to clean legal funds. In a sense this process makes it easier for law enforcement to discover the money laundering. This process is no longer a necessity within the Metaverse.

In order to regulate the Metaverse (and other online environments) new thinking needs to be generated with regard to the 'legal economy'. Remember the example given in the introduction of this book. Would you enjoy attending a virtual musical? Let us imagine that the money launderer is a fan of musicals. Instead of buying a musical ticket (and the journey around it) the launderer only needs to buy a virtual ticket. Attending a virtual concert through Metaverse can be done anonymously and without the need for conversion into a good or fiat currency. Thus raising the question of whether the "legal economy" should include virtual assets? This chapter will start with continuing the discussion on how to define the "legal economy". It

---

[1] Rechtbank Noord-Holland 05 February 2021, ECLI:NL:RBNHO:2021:1008; Gerechtshof Amsterdam 22 June 2017, ECLI:NL:GHAMS:2017:2430.

will further continue by assessing the integration phase through the Metaverse into fiat currency and physical products.

7.2 Defining the Economy

The economy is generally described as the legal and informal economy. The distinction between the legal and informal economy is drawn by a line of law.[2] The informal economy is one that is not covered by a law, yet not all informal economies are equally bad. The informal economy consists of both the informal economy and the illegal economy.[3] Both are separated from the legal economy but the degree of moral culpability is generally considered different.[4] Generally speaking society considers human trafficking of a greater moral culpability than two kids mowing the neighbor's lawn for some pocket money without filing tax returns. Thus generating a form of "grey" money and "dirty money". The launderers aim will be to promote the dirty money to either grey or the legal economy to enjoy. The key difference between the Metaverse and traditional legal economy is that of the virtual location.

The lines of legal economy and its various shades of grey with regard to the informal economy are vague. Nevertheless both these economies take place in the physical realm. The neighbor kids mowing a lawn, earn their money in a the jurisdiction where they mow the lawn. A criminal setting up a business whereby money is laundered through fictitious bills has the business located within a jurisdiction. A drug dealer buying expensive items through cash or online, conducts that purchase and receives the goods or services in a jurisdiction. The Metaverse, however, is offered through different virtual reality providers. Purchasing goods and services or establishing a firm in the Metaverse challenges the notion of jurisdiction. Jurisdiction can occur through the terms and conditions operated by the virtual reality provider. The AMLD5's main response to integration is through the regulation of exchange services. Companies or professionals who exchange virtual currencies to fiat currencies fall are regulated in the AMLD5. This response is no longer sufficient in response to MLFT, when considering the Metaverse.

In 2016 the ECB gave its opinion on the proposed AMLD5. The ECB considered

> [...]that digital currencies do not necessarily have to be exchanged into legally established currencies. They could also be used to purchase goods and services, without requiring an exchange into a legally established currency or the use of a custodial wallet provider. Such

---
[2] Ibid.
[3] Hinterseer (2002).
[4] Ibid.

7.2 Defining the Economy

transactions would not be covered by any of the control measures provided for in the proposal and could provide a means of financing illegal activities.[5]

The ECB's concern with regard to virtual assets not needing conversion to fiat currency increases through the Metaverse. Not only because it will be possible to purchase physical goods but also due to the possibility to consume virtual goods. The FATF considers a similar risk by stating "[the] *issue may become more challenging as there is greater mainstream adoption of virtual assets and the lines between virtual assets and traditional financial assets become more blurred.*"[6] The concept of what constitutes the real economy therefore needs redefining.

Generally speaking the economy is considered to be "real", consisting of assets and transactions within the physical realm. The ECB report on virtual currency schemes does not assign monetary risk to virtual currency schemes unless *real* goods and services can be purchased.[7] This type of definition might include services purchased and consumed online i.e. translation during a virtual meeting. It is however unlikely to include virtual assets. Similarly the AMLD5 considers that the virtual currencies that are exclusive to an in-game environment are not considered virtual currencies. These currencies are not considered to have any value. The virtual currencies remaining within the virtual environment remain free from supervision. The anonymity is lifted when the currency is exchanged against fiat currency. Thus providing a safety net upon MLFT.[8] This reasoning works when one considers MLFT a virtual crime with effects in the real world.[9] Arguably then by regulating the exchange facilities MLFT is prevented. This reasoning however fails if we consider virtual assets to have value as an asset to enjoy rather than to exchange.

The Metaverse realities currently in existence offer virtual concerts and other events. In addition to events the virtual reality of the Metaverse will allow for the purchase of virtual goods and services. The integration of assets into the real economy is therefore changing. There is the argument that virtual crimes cannot be considered a crime unless there are ties with the real world.[10] This argument should be considered outdated by the introduction of virtual reality. The question of virtual goods and value is often considered through a link with the real-world. Whereby value boils down to how we understand the nature of the in-world reality.[11] If the if virtual worlds are no more than playing a game the assets should not be considered a risk. Value is thus distinguished along the lines of uni and bi-directional

---

[5] OPINION OF THE EUROPEAN CENTRAL BANK of 12 October 2016 on a proposal for a directive of the European Parliament and of the Council amending Directive (EU) 2015/849 on the prevention of the use of the financial system for the purposes of money laundering or terrorist financing and amending Directive 2009/101/EC: paraf. 1.1.1.

[6] FATF (2021).

[7] European Central Bank (2012), p. 33.

[8] Visser (2017), p. 219.

[9] Chambers-Jones (2018), p. 167.

[10] Kerr (2003), pp. 372–373.

[11] Beekman (2010), p. 175.

flows. This assumption, so the article continues, rests upon the notion that all participants are there to play a game rather than monetary motivation.[12] The ties with the real world become less useful as the Metaverse develops. As the Metaverse will enable the consumption of virtual goods that may not offer a direct link to monetary values in the real world. The Dutch Supreme Court therefore considered that the forced deprivation of virtual assets constituted theft.[13] Rather than a real world or monetary approach the Supreme Court considered that the goods had real value for the possessor.[14] This real value for the possessor generates a subjective approach. The approach does not value the goods based upon a monetary claim but on a value claim. This type of reasoning would allow for the inclusion of goods and services that can no longer be valued upon fiat money. This argument is novel for legal thinking as it lets go of ties with the real world. It is economically, however, a well-accepted line of reasoning.

In 2002 economist Castranova considered with regard to virtual items, that the value was subjective and depended on the contribution to the consumers well-being.[15] If a virtual concert therefore contributes to the criminals idea of well-being, it should be considered as a reward for its criminal actions. The virtual asset is enjoyed and has therefore entered the integration phase. This should be considered true even when the asset cannot be valued upon fiat currency. This theory of subjective value is well accepted by economists as Castranova explains using the example of a diamond. Diamonds are considered highly desirable and thus highly valuable. The high price is not based upon objective characteristics but on subjective market value. This market value is accepted by economists as the objects real value.[16] Hence virtual objects can also be considered as having value, depending on the market's and individual's subjective judgement. There is however a counter argument namely that virtual items in large quantities would never bring the same satisfaction as real world assets. Yamaguchi reflected upon Castranova by creating an important distinction between the real world and virtual world economics. The difference is that the marginal utility (how much benefit the next object brings) becomes negative in the virtual reality.[17] The decrease in consumption satisfaction would suggest that a real world connection is always needed. In simpler terms a high value watch or watches would add to the feeling of status when worn in real life. In a virtual environment these luxury items would very quickly lose its status. The assumption made by Yamaguchi, however, is that the real self has more than one virtual self.[18] This assumption will no longer be true when considering the Metaverse. The Metaverse will allow the avatars to wonder throughout different

---

[12] Ibid.
[13] Hoge Raad 31 januari 2012, ECLI:NL:HR:2012:BQ9251.
[14] Ibid, r.o. 3.5.-3.6.1.
[15] Castranova (2002), p. 15.
[16] Ibid.
[17] Yamaguchi (2004).
[18] Ibid, p. 2.

worlds without the need for multiple avatars. Thus blending the digital identity with the real self. Furthermore Yamaguchi differs virtual goods from physical goods. A concert can be enjoyed fairly similarly physically and virtually. This relatively close type of consumption satisfaction blurs the line between virtual and physical consumption. The assumption that virtual items reduce in marginal utility decreases therefore no longer holds true. There is therefore ample reason to wish to regulate the sale of both physical and virtual items. In particular because it is unlikely that anonymity will be lifted from all methods of payment. The physical equivalent of anonymous currency in the real world is cash. Cash payments are regulated.

When a transaction in cash is made of €10,000 or more businesses have the obligation to conduct a due diligence investigation.[19] These businesses have no such regulations to obey. Thus the transaction supervision fully rests upon the payment structure used by the customer. As discovered in the previous sections, however, not all of the wallets currently require supervision. It is therefore risky to solely rely on wallet supervision. The current directive restricts the use of cash transactions. Cash transactions do not directly equal virtual currencies. Cash plays an important role in MLFT because it carries little tracing risk.[20] Even in the time of electronic payments cash is preferable to most MLFT. It is difficult to follow for authorities and cash does not reveal its origins.[21] Virtual currencies, even when transacted through anonymous wallets, have an encrypted ledger trail. Thus making them less attractive compared to cash. This provides argument to consider the unregulated shops less of a risk. This, however, is not a valid argument for two reasons.

The first is that there are virtual currencies that are untraceable. These are the so-called 'privacy coins'. The possibility of tracking this type of currency is currently debated. Whereby some argue that the coins can be traced, whilst others consider the tracing too complex for authorities.[22] There are however, other methods to prevent tracing.[23] It is not unlikely that technologies to avoid tracing will keep developing. The second difficulty is that legal restrictions apply for other anonymous payment methods. Anonymous prepaid cards are also restricted under AMLD5.[24] These restrictions are quite severe both in limitation and are restricted to be used

---

[19] Article 2(3) DIRECTIVE (EU) 2015/849 OF THE EUROPEAN PARLIAMENT AND OF THE COUNCIL of 20 May 2015 on the prevention of the use of the financial system for the purposes of money laundering or terrorist financing, amending Regulation (EU) No 648/2012 of the European Parliament and of the Council, and repealing Directive 2005/60/EC of the European Parliament and of the Council and Commission Directive 2006/70/EC.

[20] Schneider and Windischbauer (2008), p. 388.

[21] Riccardi and Levi (2018), p. 135.

[22] Dupuis and Gleason (2021), pp. 68–69.

[23] Ibid: 61.

[24] Article 12 Directive (EU) 2018/843 of the European Parliament and of the Council of 30 May 2018 amending Directive (EU) 2015/849 on the prevention of the use of the financial system for the purposes of money laundering or terrorist financing, and amending Directives 2009/138/EC and 2013/36/EU (Text with EEA relevance)

within the Member State of origin.[25] Therefore even if anonymous virtual currencies were brought under the scope of the Directive, such informal shops would not have to comply. The risk of MLFT, however, is present. Digital art has been suspected of facilitating MLFT,[26] traders not linked to a jurisdiction would not have to comply with any form of AMLD5. To avoid the use of dirty money at such shops the legal economy would have to cover the Metaverse. Meaning that the commerce occurring in the Metaverse should not remain an informal economy. The easiest way to achieve this by prohibiting wallets from transactions with non-regulated entities. As discussed in chapter four wallets can be restricted to only transact with other regulated wallets. Whilst possible it does not provide a comprehensive attitude towards integration of virtual assets.

It is difficult to find a single rule for how to supervise the Metaverse economy and its virtual assets. Nevertheless a good start can be made by regulating some of the companies providing virtual realities. For example KYC duties can be placed upon avatar or virtual reality providers. When an avatar wishes to own virtual assets beyond a value of a certain virtual currency threshold, the identity of the avatar should be established. Thus reducing the possibility to anonymously enjoy high value of virtual assets. Technically the question could be raised why a criminal would not create multiple accounts. Though possible this would create multiple online characters. The use of multiple online characters would reduce the marginal utility of owning the asset.[27] This reduction of pleasure derived from owning the assets makes it less attractive for criminals to view virtual assets as rewards for their crimes.

The virtual reality provider and avatar provider are not your typical obliged entities to any MLFT framework. The more standard obliged entities are banks and other financial institutions. These institutions main objective is to handle finances. The avatar and reality provider are not the type of entities that have the objective to handle financial affairs. The shift is however demonstrative of where the value would be within the Metaverse's new economy; in owning virtual assets. It is the avatar and reality providers who can supervise such ownership. Nor is the concept of placing duties of care upon those who provide a location completely new. In the Netherlands a duty of care is placed upon a landlord to prevent a weed plantation. If the landlord has neglected his/her duty of care, the cost of the administrative sanctions can be placed upon the landlord. The neglect of the duty can even result in criminal liability of the landlord.[28] This level of duty of care demonstrates that providing a space without checking for illegal activities can result in (criminal) liability. It is therefore not exceptional to consider a provider of a space liable for the activities within. Nor would it be extraordinary to consider the same to apply to a provider of a virtual space.

---

[25] Ibid.
[26] Serada, Sihvonen and Harviainen (2020), p. 461.
[27] Yamaguchi (2004).
[28] 11a Opiumwet.

As a result the economy within the Metaverse moves from a fully informal economy to a largely legal economy. By installing duties of supervision to reality and avatar providers the process of integration into the legal economy is brought back. The less wealthy avatars still participate within an informal economy. However, if a criminal wishes to enjoy a larger quantity of virtual assets he or she will have to integrate them into the formal and legal economy of the Metaverse. Thus bringing the assets back under supervision. This approach, however, only applies to integration as a virtual asset. It does not aid in the detection of physical assets purchased through virtual currency. Virtual currency is largely regulated through wallets and thus there is some level of monitoring. There are, however, two exceptions namely gaming currency and local currencies. These were not considered of high risk. With the introduction of the Metaverse this risk may change.

7.3 Value and Games

The AMLD5 includes exchange services between virtual and fiat currencies. It however exclude currencies specific to an in-game environment. The nature of this exclusion is simply the lack of risk that an in-game currency carries, there is very limited redemption value. A criminal will have little want for a virtual helmet. Yet as discussed in the second chapter the concept of games has developed into a wide variety. These includes games of fiction such as Mario Brothers and World of Warcraft but also reality based games such as Second Life and the Sims. The definition of a 'game' is not specifically given in the AMLD5. Raising the question of whether the Metaverse or parts of it could be considered a game?

Let us imagine we are playing a sci-fi game in the Metaverse. The game is provided through a specific virtual reality connected to the Metaverse. In this game you can fight aliens and explore new planets. This game allows you to both buy and earn coins. These coins can be spent in the game shop on items that are useful to the game. Let us pretend that we have bought a virtual spaceship that can be used to transport our character to a new planet within the game. So far there is very little MLFT risk. The spaceship cannot be sold or enjoyed other than within the game. Buying the spaceship is not different from buying a new level in any other game. Will that idea change however if we could bring the spaceship to our virtual homes and enjoy it as a work of art? The spaceship can now be enjoyed as a luxury good or item of status. Perhaps I can transfer the spaceship to another avatar in return for virtual currency. Though the spaceship is still intended for the same purpose (accessing a new planet in the game), the risk of MLFT has increased by facilitating the transfer of the spaceship to my virtual home. What if in addition to a virtual spaceship the company would send me a physical miniature? A miniature that I can then sell for fiat currency. The risk of MLFT further increases even though the initial currency earned was technically exclusive to the game environment. The scenario may seem unrealistic, it is however not the first time that gaming currency has proven to be more MLFT risky than expected.

The hyperinflation in Venezuela provide an interesting case study with regard to gaming currencies. To avoid the hyperinflation, Venezuelans started using gold from the game RuneScape. The gold is based upon a centralized ledger and is technically exclusive to a game environment. The preamble of AMLD5 excludes "[...] *in-games currencies, that can be used exclusively within a specific game environment.*"[29] These currencies are considered to be of low risk due to their value being limited to the virtual reality of the game. Due to the popularity of the game black markets have occurred where these assets are traded. These black markets facilitated the trade between ORS and dollars which aided the Venezuelan population in storing value. The same black markets have, however, also been linked to large scale MLFT practices.[30] In this case the Venezuelans still had to transfer their gaming currency to dollars. As discussed in the previous chapter, however, these currencies can be used to purchase actual goods. The gaming currency then can be used to purchase physical objects without need for conversion.

Earlier research has therefore argued that when a virtual asset can be transferred within a game, there is the risk of a black market. The game provider should therefore have monitoring duties under the AML framework, unless the provider can prevent a black market.[31] Practically the game provider will therefore either monitor transactions to ban players suspected of selling their game currency, or monitoring and reporting suspicious transactions to the national supervisor.[32] Unfortunately to date there is no supervisory framework in place for such game currencies. In the EU neither game providers nor the exchange offices are monitored.[33] The more popular the gaming environment, the more efficient the gaming currency can act as a complementary currency.[34] Participating in these black markets is generally against the contract with the game provider.

Most game developers will have terms and agreements on selling assets outside of the game. Despite these terms and agreements there is little enforcement. The main reason is that enforcement is expensive for game developers. Sometimes costing op to millions in order to prosecute a single violator.[35] Private enforcement is only a real option if the benefits outweigh the costs, meaning that the costs must be able to be redressed from the perpetrator.[36] With the current enforcement costs it is unlikely a private individual would be able to pay such damages. The enforcement costs, however, could be limited in the Metaverse. Current enforcement costs are

---

[29] Preamble 10.
[30] Cuthbertson (2019).
[31] Mooij (2022).
[32] Ibid.
[33] Ibid.
[34] Petri et al. (2010), pp. 141–152.
[35] Press release Banner Witcoff, 'Banner & Witcoff Wins Video Game Lawsuit for RuneScape Developer Jagex, Ltd.', 3 februari 2012, https://bannerwitcoff.com/banner-witcoff-wins-video-game-lawsuit-for-runescape-developer-jagex-ltd.
[36] Becker and Stigler (1974), p. 14.

high due to the anonymity of gaming participants. If Metaverse avatar users are verified this may reduce enforcement costs. This would, however require all avatars to be verified. It is therefore likely that enforcement will be difficult to discover for private parties. Thus to prevent MLFT occurring through games, public laws are necessary.

The Metaverse already features immersive games. Gaming experts consider that the games that can be offered through the Metaverse will be hugely popular.[37] The gaming rewards are difficult to define. The first approach is that all gaming currencies are virtual currencies and the gaming providers will have to classify as wallet providers. The problem with this approach is that it makes it difficult for small start-ups to comply with the regulation. A second approach is to continuously scan for black markets and only when such a market exists, consider the gaming currency to be virtual currency. With regard to MLFT this strategy may be very effective as black markets form the largest risk of MLFT. The question, however, is who would assess the existence of black markets? With regard to the Metaverse a similar approach can be used as to the virtual assets. Players below a certain value can be left unverified but players above a certain value must be verified and monitored. The verification, however, would only be necessary when the assets can be transferred from one player to another or when the assets could be brough outside the virtual reality space of the game. The value of the account at which verification is necessary would need to reflect the (economic) risk of MLFT.

In addition to the complexity of value regulation with regard to games, the Metaverse will offer local currencies. These local currencies provide further complexity as they are exempted from the AMLD5.

7.4 Local Use

The AMLD5 furthermore excludes "[l]*ocal currencies, also known as complementary currencies, that are used in very limited networks such as a city or a region and among a small number of users should not be considered to be virtual currencies.*"[38] This excludes local currencies currently set-up by cities. There is a rising tendencies among cities to introduce their own currency. These currencies can vary from physical notes such as in Deltebre in Spain[39] to cryptocurrency such as those introduced in Hull[40] and the U.S.[41] The coins have different intentions but generally share certain characteristics. Citizens can earn their coins by volunteer work, spending at local shops or are given the coins as (part of) social welfare. The coins can

---

[37] Patterson and Bidar (2022).
[38] Preamble 11.
[39] Altenhenne (2022).
[40] O'Geran (2020).
[41] City Coins. Miami Coin. https://www.citycoins.co/miamicoin.

generally only be redeemed at local shops. The local coins are generally considered not a high MLFT risk. These coins can best be compared to a loyalty programme. Both city coins and loyalty programmes are generally earned through consumption with local shops. The redemption value is generally limited. It is therefore argued that both placement and extraction is difficult.[42] The similarities between the city coins and the loyalty programmes create a low MLFT risk. The risks can change as the city coins change. In particular the definition of a "city" can change. A city coin local to Deltebre can be considered of low risk. The total population of the whole municipality is around 11,500 people. The people receiving the coins are those on social welfare within the municipality. They can spend these coins with the local shops. This system therefore aims to promote both the welfare of those on social benefits and of the local shopkeepers. With this low redemption rate it is unlikely there is a high level of MLFT. Furthermore the local shopkeepers receiving the coins primarily hand them in to the municipality for euros. The risk of MLFT is thus very low but let's compare this to the Hull coin. The Hull coin was intended to serve the local welfare of Hull. Whereby citizens could earn their coins based upon positive actions such as quitting smoking or volunteering. The coins could then be spent in the local shops. The amount of citizens in Hull area is around 320,000 who could all earn and spend these coins. The result was not only a major scam[43] but also a lively trade in the coin. The coin was established on very similar principles to that of Deltebre but due to its size carries a higher MLFT risk. Both coins would however likely qualify as local virtual currency. Thus raising the question when is something local?

The expected realities in the Metaverse are likely to be diverse. Whereby some virtual realities might focus on providing a gaming scenario. Another virtual reality provider may provide a virtual shopping street. The virtual shopping street can play host to a range of shops from various locations. If each shop uses its own (crypto) currency, it can be confusing for consumers. To enhance customer experience, the virtual location could introduce its own currency. The resulting scenario would be that close to that of the game Second Life where Linden Dollars were the going currency within the reality. As discussed in Chap. 3, Linden Labs, the developer of Second Life, had the transactions occur through its subsidiary Tilia. Tilia is a registered money transmitter with the US supervisor. The question is whether the same will apply to a virtual reality provider who introduces its own, local, currency.

If we imagine the currency can be used in the shopping street when is it still local? The region where the currency can be spent is limited to a single Metaverse reality. It is therefore different from general cryptocurrencies which can be spent in various Metaverse realities and beyond. Unlike local city coins, however, the currency can be spent in shops that are virtually confined to a street but physically can be located throughout the globe. Furthermore the virtual reality can be accessed by a high number of people located all over the world. The definition of a region as used by the

---

[42] Supr n. 64,392.
[43] Marinoff (2016).

AMLD5 is therefore given a new dimension. The second criterion for exclusion is that of used by a small number of users. Little is written on when the criteria for exclusion are no longer met. Considering the complexity of the accessibility with regard to the term 'region', it would be preferable to exclude small economies. As with the gaming environment legislating according to physical counterparts seems obsolete. Rather than examine whether something can be used in a region, the legislator should evaluate the size of the economy in that currency. Perhaps even giving a threshold as to when something is used in "a very limited network". In addition the legislator should examine how the coins are obtained. I.e. are they unique to an avatar or can they be transferred between wallets?

7.5 Conclusion and Recommendations

Though it is difficult to legislate in terms of 'placement' and 'integration' it is not impossible. The legislative framework will however have to change its approach. The first is with regard to how to define the legal economy. The legal economy should be detached from the physical economy. Virtual assets can be enjoyed as much as real assets. The concept that all virtual assets need conversion has largely and will furthermore become obsolete. This change in focus closely relates to what was discussed in chapter four with regard to legislating the intention. The intention for MLFT is to obtain an asset that can be enjoyed. Enjoyment can be considered to as an object useful to commit the crime and as an asset as reward for the crime. The current concept of a reward is an asset in the physical world but with the Metaverse this no longer holds true. Therefore the Metaverse needs to become part of the legislated (and therefore formal) economy.

Secondly through the Metaverse virtual currencies that seem worthless can gain value very quickly. This applies to both gaming currencies and local or regional currencies. Rather than excluding them from the legal framework the valuable coins should be included. That means that the legislator will have to, again, look at intention. Can a coin be reasonably used for MLFT? If so the virtual currency should be included in the legislative framework. This could be best achieved through some value thresholds. If a certain amount of users are using the currency or if users wish to obtain a large amount, then due diligence duties apply to the issuer of the local coin. Some of these cut-off lines might be fairly arbitrary i.e. a user wishing to own a value of 9,999 coins may not be monitored but one with 10,000 coins might. Nevertheless these values are necessary to create clarity and are not different from cash declarations or suspicious transactions above a similar threshold.

These adjustments aim to respond to the virtual economy. Thereby creating a framework that is adept to the traditional three phases of MLFT and the Metaverse. As discussed in the third chapter there are three risks specific to the Metaverse. One of these risks, non-EU transactions, has been discussed in Chap. 4. The second and third, anonymity and NFTs, will be discussed in the next chapter.

References

Altenhenne M (2022) Some Spanish municipalities introduce their own currency. *DW* 22 february online available at: https://www.dw.com/en/some-spanish-municipalities-introduce-their-own-currency/av-60870840

Becker GS, Stigler GJ (1974) Law enforcement, malfeasance, and compensation of enforcers. J Leg Stud 1

Beekman N (2010) Virtual assets, real tax: the capital gains/ordinary income distinction in virtual worlds. Columb Sci Technol Law Rev 11(152)

Castranova E (2002) On virtual economics. Available at SSRN: https://ssrn.com/abstract=338500

Chambers-Jones C (2018) Money laundering in a virtual world. In: King C, Walker C, Gurulé J (eds) The Palgrave handbook of criminal and terrorism financing law. Palgrave, Cham

Cuthbertson A (13 January 2019) How children playing Fortnite are helping to fuel organised crime. The Independent

Dupuis D, Gleason K (2021) Money laundering with cryptocurrency: open doors and the regulatory dialectic. J Financ Crime 28(1)

European Central Bank (2012) Virtual Currency Schemes. Frankfurt. https://www.ecb.europa.eu/pub/pdf/other/virtualcurrencyschemes201210en.pdf

FATF (2021) Second 12-Month review of the revised FATF standards on virtual assets and virtual asset service providers. Paris

Hinterseer K (2002) Criminal finance: the political economy of money laundering in a comparative legal context. Kluwer, The Hague

Kerr O (2003) The problem of perspective in internet law. Georgetown Law J 91

Marinoff N (2016) Hullcoin leads this week's digital currency news. Bitcoinist.com

Mooij A (2022) Toezicht op virtuele valuta: de wereld van het gamen. SEW Tijdschrift voor Europees en economisch recht 3

O'Geran L (2020) HullCoin- how hull is using blockchain for good. Bristol Pound. Online available at: https://bristolpound.org/hullcoin/; https://themerkle.com/the-city-of-hull-seemingly-has-its-own-cryptocurrency/

Patterson D, Bidar M (2022) You've heard of the metaverse. Here's what it looks like. CBS News 03 March

Petri I, Rana O, Silaghi G (2010) SLA as a complementary currency in Peer-2-peer markets. In: Altmann K, Rana O (eds) Economics of grids, clouds, systems, and services. Springer, Berlin

Riccardi M, Levi M (2018) Cash, crime and anti-money laundering. In: King C, Walker C, Gurulé J (eds) The Palgrave handbook of criminal and terrorism financing law. Palgrave Macmillan, Cham

Schneider F, Windischbauer U (2008) Money laundering: some facts. Eur. J Law Econ 26:387–404

Serada A, Sihvonen T, Harviainen J (2020) *CryptoKitties* and the new ludic economy: how blockchain introduces value, ownership and scarcity in digital gaming. Games Culture 16(4)

Visser S (2017) Nieuwe witwastypologieën in de strijd tegen witwassen met virtuele betaalmiddelen. TBS&H 2017: 4

Yamaguchi H (2004) An analysis of virtual currencies in online games. Available at SSRN: https://ssrn.com/abstract=544422

Open Access This chapter is licensed under the terms of the Creative Commons Attribution 4.0 International License (http://creativecommons.org/licenses/by/4.0/), which permits use, sharing, adaptation, distribution and reproduction in any medium or format, as long as you give appropriate credit to the original author(s) and the source, provide a link to the Creative Commons license and indicate if changes were made.

The images or other third party material in this chapter are included in the chapter's Creative Commons license, unless indicated otherwise in a credit line to the material. If material is not included in the chapter's Creative Commons license and your intended use is not permitted by statutory regulation or exceeds the permitted use, you will need to obtain permission directly from the copyright holder.

Chapter 8
Non-fungible Tokens and Stateless Firms

8.1 Non-fungible Tokens

Non-Fungible Tokens (NFTs) are difficult to define legally. As discussed in Chap. 3, NFTs are a digital form of ownership certificate. The digital ownership can be of various items such as collector goods, arts and land. Whilst NFTs have practical value they are also associated with MLFT.[1] The use of NFTs in the Metaverse is likely to be widespread as Metaverse itself offers its own NFT trading and generating system.[2] The NFTs can be used to own land in the Metaverse or exclusive ownership of art used to decorate virtual realities. The following paragraphs will therefore discuss how to regulate NFTs. In particular whether these should be regulated as a virtual currency or according to their physical counterparts.

The NFT is not quickly associated with currency as it represents ownership of an asset. It is therefore questionable if NFTs meet the criteria of a virtual currency. In particular that of a digital representation of value that is accepted as a means of exchange. It is easy to argue that a NFT has value, but that does not make it an accepted means of exchange. A car has value, yet it is unlikely a consumer will use it as means of exchange when buying groceries. The concept of value within the functional properties of a currency is that it is fungible. Jevons argued in 1875 that fungible currency was economically more beneficial than payment systems through barter.[3] This concept of fungibility is still considered valid today.[4] If this definition of value is used, NFTs would not be considered a virtual currency. By definition a NFT cannot be divided, thus not classifying as currency. It is likely that value should be determined according to the functional definition of money. Meaning that a token would have to be fungible in order to classify as a virtual currency. The main basis

---

[1] Sharma et al. (2022).
[2] Metaverse (2022) Homepage. https://mvs.org/.
[3] Jevons (1875).
[4] Berentsen and Rocheteau (2002).

for this argument is the definition given by the Financial Action Task Force (FATF). The FATF uses the same definition for virtual assets and virtual currencies. It defines both assets and currencies as "[...] *functions as (1) a medium of exchange; and/or (2) a unit of account; and/or (3) a store of value* [...]".[5] The use of a single definition for both assets and currency, suggests a broad definition for value. The inclusion of medium of exchange, unit of account and/or store of value, however, directs towards a more functional approach to value. Instinctively it is difficult to define NFTs as money. NFTs represent commodities rather than a currency. Fairfield therefore suggests classifying NFTs in a similar fashion as the physical counterpart they represent.[6] Certainly from a legal certainty point of view this type of classification has merit. Particularly when the NFT is used to guarantee ownership and the parties disagree on the execution of the contract. This type of classification would provide tools to answer questions on jurisdiction and what legal principles should apply. Such a classification, however, creates uncertainty with regard to the wallets that store the NFTs and a potential loophole with regard to AMLD5. The NFTs themselves can prove ownership and thereby can replace legal fictions such as the posser is expected to be owner. This type of certificate of authenticity is clearly not a currency similar to fungible coins. There is thus ample reason not to classify them as virtual currency. So why bother?

The NFTs, however, represent value stored in the digital wallet. The value is technically related to the object it represents. However, it can be easily generated and used as a messaging system. The digital wallet used to store an NFT is the same as those used to store other virtual currencies. If not supervised the result would be a two-fold loophole. Firstly a provider focusing on NFT storage would therefore be able to avoid supervisory oversight by stating its business is storing NFT, rather than virtual currencies. This situation is highly unwanted. Secondly as Fairfield describes the NFT can represent the deeds to i.e. land.[7] He therefore argues that NFTs should be considered personal property and the law of sales should apply.[8] Physical real estate transactions are considered part of the types of transactions that involve MLFT.[9] A physical land transaction would, therefore, normally be transacted through a notary or solicitor. These professions are covered under the AMLD5.[10] The law of a real estate transaction will generally be determined by the country where it is physically located. The question is under what, if any, jurisdiction would a plot in the Metaverse be located? Could virtual reality providers determine how sales are conducted? Furthermore the value of virtual real estate varies greatly.

---

[5] FATF Report (2014), p. 4.
[6] Fairfield (2021), p. 55.
[7] Ibid.
[8] Ibid.
[9] Remeur (2019).
[10] Article 2(3) sub b.

One of the Metaverse realities currently in existence is Decentraland. Plots of Decentraland currently trade at $6000 per plot.[11] This market is furthermore rapidly rising.[12] The idea that virtual assets are less valuable than physical assets no longer applies to all cases. However, in other virtual realities plots of lands may be worth a fraction of the plots in Decentraland. To require a solicitor to assist in the purchase of a virtual plot of land worth €10,- seems excessive. Similarly in the United States NFTs are (likely) supervised through the National Defense Authorization Act.[13] It however is not clear whether an NFT should be considered as the sale of an "antiquity" or a cryptocurrency. Leading some to fear for an aggressive enforcement theories.[14] The opposite is, however, also possible namely that of no enforcement. To avoid regulatory oversight it would be the most straightforward to classify an NFT as a virtual currency. The wallets would then monitor NFTs entering and leaving the wallet as if it were cryptocurrency. Though intuitively it would be odd to consider NFTs currency, it is not economically odd to consider commodities as currency.

The first criterion for money is that of a medium of exchange. It has to be accepted as a form of payment. This criterion flows forth from the concept of "double coincidence of wants".[15] A problem that occurs in barter transactions. If I want apples and have pears I would need to find someone who would want pears and has apples. If the opposing party only has nectarines then the transaction would not occur. Money can solve this issue through universal acceptance. NFTs represent objects, therefore if two parties conduct a transaction whereby an NFT is traded against a service it would be considered barter. However this need not be the case. The EBA considers that the term value can also refer to a form of commodity.[16] Economic research has furthermore argued that goods can be considered a medium of exchange. Currencies can take the form of commodities through intrinsic properties and extrinsic beliefs.[17] A particularly popular example of commodity currency are cigarettes. Cigarettes served as commodity in Germany after the war.[18] Whilst there are various examples of commodity currencies they are not always present in complex economies. Commodity currencies rise due to the lack of money and trade higher in value than its utility value. When (fiat) money is introduced commodity currency is crowded out.[19] The Metaverse is likely to have various options of non-commodity currency provided on the blockchain. Though it could be argued

---

[11] Dowling (2022), p. 1.

[12] Ibid, p. 4.

[13] H.R.6395 – William M. (Mac) Thornberry National Defense Authorization Act for Fiscal Year 2021, available at: https://www.congress.gov/bill/116th-congress/house-bill/6395.

[14] Sauter et al. (2021).

[15] Jevons (1875).

[16] European Banking Authority (2014), p. 11.

[17] Kiyotaki and Wright (1989).

[18] Senn (1951).

[19] Burdett et al. (2001), pp. 117–142.

that cryptocurrencies should not be considered viable currencies due to the, often extreme, price fluctuations. Whilst the initial cryptocurrencies fluctuated in value, newer currencies such as stable coins are pegged to a fiat currency and their value is relatively stable. It is therefore unlikely that there is a great need for a commodity value. Secondly due to the complex economy of the Metaverse it is difficult to use NFTs as a unit of account.

The criterion of unit of account is to demonstrate the value difference between goods and services.[20] It allows a potential customer to distinguish the price attached to different objects. The difficulty with NFTs is that their value depends upon the considered value of the object it represents. NFT1 does not necessarily have the same value as NFT2. NFTs can furthermore fluctuate heavily in value. Thus making it difficult to store value, which is the third criterion for currency. The same price fluctuations, however, are true for bitcoin. Bitcoin can therefore also be considered not to fulfill the store of value criterion.[21] Nevertheless bitcoin and other cryptocurrencies are perceived as currency.[22] Despite the difficulty in its store of value bitcoin, however, can be exchanged against other cryptocurrencies and fiat currencies. NFTs, however, have to be sold rather than exchanged. Whilst from a regulatory point of view it would be straightforward to consider NFTs as virtual currency, it seems unlikely they will qualify as such. The qualification of NFTs according to their physical counterpart seems equally risky. Not only because it risk lack of jurisdiction but also because it may stifle the Metaverse economy. Considering the ease of monitoring NFTs through the wallets it is recommendable to change the legal definition of a wallet provider. Rather than the term 'virtual currency' the FATF's term 'virtual asset' seems preferable whereby virtual asset should be interpreted as a commodity or currency. The wallet can then supervise the currency and NFTs within.

8.2 Stateless Firms

Anonymity is a particularly interesting risk with regard to the Metaverse and virtual reality in general. The previous chapters have discussed due diligence and customer verification duties in the three stages of MLFT. Specific to the Metaverse, however, will be the possibility of anonymous companies. The physical counterparts of anonymous companies are shell corporations. Shell corporations have a significant role in the process of MLFT. These corporations hide their true owner. Thus providing a disconnect between the owner and the illegal transfers.[23] The EU response to the anonymity of the shell corporations is through the UBO registry.

---

[20] Mattke et al. (2020), p. 29.
[21] Kubát (2015), pp. 409–416.
[22] Mattke et al. (2020).
[23] der Does de Willebois et al. (2011), p. 26.

8.2 Stateless Firms

The UBO registry contains the information on who controls and owns the corporation or trust. The AMLD4 set the ownership indication at above 25% of shares owned directly or indirectly by the same legal person(s).[24] There has been some discussion as to whether setting exact ownership limits is the right direction,[25] and whether privacy is safeguarded. It is too early to tell whether the UBO is effective,[26] nevertheless the registry seems to decrease the possibility for shell corporations within the EU to hide their owners. The duty to register is based upon the nationality of the legal person. The obvious risk are those companies not located within the EU. The EU, however, does not have any jurisdiction to regulate the companies outside its own territory. The transactions to companies with less regulatory obligations are part of the subjective MLFT risk criteria. The system whilst not flawless improves the regulation of these companies. The regulatory obligations within the EU are furthermore based upon FATF recommendations.[27] Thus the best approach for the EU (and FATF) is to promote international compliance with these regulatory recommendations. The Metaverse brings similar risks of being able to transact with countries in various jurisdictions. These will have to register with the UBO registry within their own jurisdiction. Companies providing digital services are not exempt from registration, depending on where they are incorporated these firms will have to register with their respective UBO. The Metaverse, however, transforms the concept of a shell corporation into a completely new risk; namely that of stateless firms.

The nationality of an economic entity is generally determined through its foundation within a jurisdiction. The entity generates legal personality by its establishment as (limited)company. It needs this legal personality to purchase goods, open a bank account and use other services. If no legal personality is generated the economic activities can be run on a personal title. The nationality of the company is then equal to the nationality of the person. The legal personality of the company is the primary criterion to determine the applicable legislative framework. The Metaverse creates an opportunity for companies to exist without nationality. Virtual reality providers could demand that any economic entity is registered as such with a national supervisor. There are however ways to circumvent such requirements. The economic entity can either find a provider that does not require registration as a (legal) person or by creating its own virtual reality. The easy solution would be to consider such entities sole traders. Sole traders, however, are physically present somewhere and can generally be linked to their business. Generally speaking sole traders will have acquired a bank account which links them to the business. Within the Metaverse it will be extremely difficult to establish the person behind the laptop.

---

[24] Article 3(6) under a, Directive (EU) 2015/849 of the European Parliament and of the Council of 20 May 2015 on the prevention of the use of the financial system for the purposes of money laundering or terrorist financing, amending Regulation (EU) No 648/2012 of the European Parliament and the Council, and repealing Directive 2005/60/EC of the European Parliament and the Council and Commission Directive 2006/70/EC, Art 2 (2).

[25] Daudrikh (2021), pp. 140–141.

[26] the registry had to be completed on the 27th of March 2022.

[27] Daudrikh (2021).

Furthermore as previously discussed through the use of virtual currencies it will be easy to set-up an anonymous wallet and enter the economic framework. Without incorporation into a jurisdiction and being able to link the person to the entity the result is a virtual stateless company.

The difficulty with stateless companies is that they can provide full anonymity to its beneficiaries as there is no government entity responsible for their supervision. The lack of supervision and jurisdiction increases the risk of MLFT. The phenomenon of stateless firms is not entirely new. Irish incorporated entities could declare their profits as part of a headquarter located in an tax-free jurisdiction. Thereby avoiding paying tax in both Ireland and abroad. This concept was referred to as that of stateless firms.[28] Whilst these firms were considered stateless they were only stateless with regard to taxation. The firms still existed and contained legal personality. In order to reduce tax avoidance, countries have generated approaches to determine where a company is located despite its incorporation. These approaches may help determine where the virtual companies are located.

The first approach is whereby location is determined through incorporation into its jurisdiction. This was discussed in the previous paragraph will not be a likely solution for the Metaverse. The second approach is based upon where the company generates its products. To reduce the amount of stateless firms in Ireland the government approach is through a 'place of incorporation' test.[29] This approach considered where the activities and in particular management and control of the company is located.[30] This approach in the physical world led to serious tax avoidance.[31] It may, however, form a good approach to establish nationality of online firms. If a company is stateless, its nationality can be determined according to where it conducts its activities. If the virtual reality has a jurisdiction (clause) attached to it, the same jurisdiction would apply to the company. The problem with this approach, however, is that not all virtual realities will be attached to a jurisdiction and persons (or management) may not always be traceable. With regard to the production of physical goods, this is assuming there are physical goods rather than virtual, it might be difficult to trace (though not impossible). The question is whether efforts will be made to trace the production location and by whom. Governments are unlikely to spend resources on tracing a company without clear indication that their economic entity is harmful to their economy. The Commission may spent such resources when the company has ties to the EU. As the Commission may in the future claim residual tax leftovers.[32] But momentarily this legislation for

---

[28] Stateless companies – Ireland's position clarified. A&L Goodbody, 2013 October 24. Available at: https://www.lexology.com/library/detail.aspx?g=1637cf1e-dba4-4e4e-8339-7b8d2f5d476c.

[29] Quinn et al. (2013).

[30] Barrera and Bustamante (2018), p. 153.

[31] Ibid.

[32] European Commission Press release: The Commission proposes the next generation of EU own resources. 22 December 2021. Available at: https://ec.europa.eu/commission/presscorner/detail/en/ip_21_7025.

tax is still within a draft version. Secondly the company's activities may be fully virtual, i.e. the production of virtual shoes for Avatars. Its economic activities may therefore not perse be linked to physical jurisdiction. To award companies nationalities through a top-down approach may therefore not always be possible. It is therefore this researchers recommendation to establish a bottom-up approach through wallet regulation.

The virtual economic entity may not need to have a legal personality to purchase real estate or limit risk. It will need some form of currency. The due diligence of a wallet would therefore include establishing the identity of their customer. Whereby the wallet would have to establish the UBO of the economic entity. Economic entities without legal personality should be refused service. Currently, however, the due diligence of a company is limited to reasonable measures.[33] If customer verification could not take place, transactions are only considered suspicious if there are other indications of MLFT.[34] This level of due diligence is not necessarily suited to prevent stateless entities from gaining access to wallets. The customer due diligence should at least include the verification of the companies existence. If the legal existence of a company cannot be verified, the company should be excluded access. The alternative would be to wait to see if transactions could be considered suspicious. However, if the entity's nationality cannot be determined investigation will become increasingly difficult and costly. Raising the same question as to whether the investigation will be carried out. Wallets should therefore only provide services or sell their software to clients with a verified legal personality.

References

Barrera R, Bustamante J (2018) The rotten apple: taks avoidance in Ireland. Int Trade J 32(1)
Berentsen A, Rocheteau G (2002) On the efficiency of monetary exchange: how divisibility of money matters. J Monet Econ 8:1621–1649
Burdett K, Trejos A, Wright R (2001) Cigarette Money. J Econ Theory 99:117–142
Daudrikh Y (2021) Beneficial owner central registry as a tool to fight money laundering and terrorist financing. Financ Law Rev 24(4)
der Does de Willebois V et al (2011) Puppet masters. How the corrupt use legal structures to hide stolen assets and what to do about it. World Bank Publications, Landover
Dowling M (2022) Fertile LAND: pricing non-fungible tokens. Financ Res Lett 44:102096
European Banking Authority (2014) Opinion on 'Virtual Currencies'. Frankfurt. https://www.eba.europa.eu/sites/default/documents/files/documents/10180/657547/81409b94-4222-45d7-ba3b-7deb5863ab57/EBA-Op-2014-08%20Opinion%20on%20Virtual%20Currencies.pdf?retry=1
Fairfield J (2021) Runaway technology. Can the law keep up? Cambridge University Press, Cambridge
FATF Report (2014) Virtual currencies. Key definitions and potential AML/CFT risks. Paris. Available at: http://www.fatf-gafi.org/media/fatf/documents/reports/Virtual-currency-key-definitions-and-potential-aml-cft-risks.pdf

---

[33] Snijder-Kuipers and Godlieb (2022), paraf. 7.3.4.
[34] Ibid.

Jevons W (1875) Money and the mechanism of exchange. New York: Appleton 1875, online available https://oll.libertyfund.org/title/jevons-money-and-the-mechanism-of-exchange#lf0191_head_004

Kiyotaki N, Wright R (1989) On money as a medium of exchange. J Polit Econ 97(4)

Kubát M (2015) Virtual currency bitcoin in the scope of money definition and store of value. Proc Econ Finance 30

Mattke J, Maier C, Reis L (2020) Is cryptocurrency money? Three empirical studies analyzing medium of exchange, store of value and unit of account. SIGMIS-CPR, June 19–21, Nuremberg: 29

Quinn A, Fogarty W, Miller E (2013) Ireland: Irish law changes for 'Stateless' companies – preparing for the future. Mondaq 29 October. Available at: https://www.mondaq.com/ireland/corporate-tax/271816/irish-law-changes-for-39stateless39-companies-preparing-for-the-future

Remeur C (2019) Understanding money laundering through real estate transactions. European Parliament Briefing, Brussel. Available at: https://www.europarl.europa.eu/cmsdata/161094/7%20-%2001%20EPRS_Understanding%20money%20laundering%20through%20real%20estate%20transactions.pdf

Sauter B, Ortes M, Levinson L (2021) How NFTs could trigger lawsuits and anti-money laundering regulation. Forkast

Senn P (1951) Cigarettes as currency. J Financ 6(3)

Sharma T et al (2022) "It's A Blessing and A Curse": unpacking creators' practices with non-fungible tokens (NFTs) and their communities. Available at: https://doi.org/10.1145/nnnnnnn.nnnnnnn

Snijder-Kuipers B, Godlieb A (2022) Mislukt cliëntonderzoek. O&R: 131

Open Access This chapter is licensed under the terms of the Creative Commons Attribution 4.0 International License (http://creativecommons.org/licenses/by/4.0/), which permits use, sharing, adaptation, distribution and reproduction in any medium or format, as long as you give appropriate credit to the original author(s) and the source, provide a link to the Creative Commons license and indicate if changes were made.

The images or other third party material in this chapter are included in the chapter's Creative Commons license, unless indicated otherwise in a credit line to the material. If material is not included in the chapter's Creative Commons license and your intended use is not permitted by statutory regulation or exceeds the permitted use, you will need to obtain permission directly from the copyright holder.

Chapter 9
Conclusion

The Metaverse will provide us with new opportunities to enjoy the internet. Through the Metaverse society can enjoy the internet in 3D. This brings new ways to interact and is creating new economies. The possibilities of the Metaverse to facilitate social interactions and to create more affordable luxuries are endless. Unfortunately there is also a dark side to the possibilities. Where there are good intentions there are also bad intentions. The Metaverse is already full of them. The combination of anonymous, fast and without the need for third party international payments risks money laundering and the financing of terrorism. This book has discussed the precise risks of MLFT with regard to the Metaverse and the adeptness of the current regulatory framework.

It was first established that within the traditional three phases of placement, layering and integration there are several risks specific to the Metaverse. The first phase of placement describes how illicit funds are entered into the economy. Particular risks in relation to the Metaverse are the wallets and the smart contracts. Especially the wide variety of different wallets available is cause for concern. The wallets are necessary to store virtual currency and can be offered as a single service or as part of a package of services. To define a wallet the law uses the word "entity" this term is broad enough to cover wallets offered both as a package and as a single service. The problem however is that the AMLD5 then divides the wallets into two categories the custodian wallets and the non-custodian wallets. The non-custodian wallets are those that store virtual currencies without saving the keys needed to transact the currency. There is therefore no third party that can monitor the transactions from and into the wallet. It is for this reason that the legislator has decided to exclude this category from supervision. Thus creating a system of wallets that is not supervised. This book has discovered that the law is outdated in its focus on human supervision. Rather this book suggests that wallets perform transactions through software connected to the internet. This software can be equipped with customer identification and an algorithm that detects suspicious transactions. The algorithm can be connected to the national supervisor. Through the use of XAI the algorithm can provide both notice of suspicious transactions and explanatory reports to the national supervisor. This approach reduces the need for human supervision and can thereby include non-custodian wallets. The second risk with regard to the placement phase of the Metaverse is that of smart contracts. Smart contracts can automatically execute an instruction. The use of smart contracts can automate the process of entering small amounts of value into or to a wallet in order to avoid detection. The process of placing small funds into the system to avoid detection is called smurfing or structuring. Smurfing used to entail a labor intensive process. Whilst the process is facilitated by the use of smart contracts these contracts have to be connected to wallets. It is therefore recommendable that smart contracts above a value threshold are reported as suspicious by the monitoring algorithm in the wallet. Technically thresholds can be avoided too by creating more wallets and smart contracts. There is no way to completely avoid this risk, only to mitigate it. By supervising the smart contracts the process of smurfing becomes more difficult and labor intensive. This mitigates and reduces ease of undetected smurfing.

The second phase of MLFT is that of layering. Layering is the process of hiding the criminal origins of the funds. In particular challenges lay with the different types of virtual currency that are available and the different structural characteristics. Unsupervised currencies can be used to transact and create a layer between the criminal origin of the funds and the resulting funds. The definition of a virtual currency excludes all currencies guaranteed or issued by central banks or governments. This part of the definition becomes an issue with regard to cryptocurrencies that are recognized as legal tender. Furthermore the definition of a virtual currency is based upon those currencies that are based upon a blockchain. There are however cases whereby currencies are not based upon blockchains but are centralized. Even if these centralized virtual currencies were to fall under the definition of a virtual currency the legal framework does not cover the role of the issuer. A centralized currency is issued by a private party. This issuer can either manage all facets of the payment technology including wallet and exchange services or allow third-parties to offer such services. In comparison a central bank as an issuer of fiat currency has no specific obligations to monitor their transactions. The commercial banks perform the monitoring functions. Considering the structural differences between the centralized virtual currencies it is recommended that a monitoring framework is agreed upon with the national supervisor. The centralized virtual currencies demonstrate another problem namely that they can be created for specific (gaming)environments.

These gaming environments are left unregulated by the AMLD5 because a currency specific to a single environment carries little risk. The difficulty, however, is that the Metaverse will present an environment whereby the boundaries are difficult to define. This new virtual environment creates risks with regard to the third phase of MLFT; integration. With the disappearance of the traditional boundaries the traditional of the economy changes. What is a game and what is a virtual environment that brings real enjoyment? The enjoyment of virtual assets creates a scenario whereby the exchange of virtual assets into fiat or physical assets is no longer needed. This book therefore argues that instead of focusing on physical assets the definition of the economy should focus on subjective value. If a virtual asset can be enjoyed and transferred it should be considered to have economic value. This

9 Conclusion

virtual economy is left unsupervised. A user who wants to own large quantities of virtual assets can do so without supervision. Therefore virtual assets are attractive to criminals. In order to adapt the legal framework to the virtual economy this book recommends increased monitoring. Specifically virtual reality and avatar providers should be obliged to verify there customers in case of high-level accounts. This type of increased monitoring on online asset ownership creates a formal and informal online economy. The existence of an informal virtual economy is not morally bad perse if it is small enough to avoid criminal activity. A similar issue that the virtual economy will face is the question to what is local? Local currencies are exempted from the legal framework. Local in the physical world is difficult to define, should a city with a million people be considered local? The virtual local, however, can be accessed globally and by millions of users. Nevertheless the currency can be limited to a virtual area. The legislator should therefore provide clear standards to what constitutes as local and increase its focus on the criterion of "very limited network of users". A threshold may be considered arbitrary but it avoids confusion. The definition of very limited is vague and leaves room for avoiding the supervisory framework.

The adaptation of the regulatory framework to the three traditional phases of MLFT is however not enough. The Metaverse will present new challenges such as Non-Fungible Tokens (NFTs) and the possibility of stateless firms. The NFT is a strange creature as it is not designed to function as a currency. It represents a certificate of ownership and carries the value of owning an item. The item can differ from real-estate to art and anything in between. The NFTs are linked to large scale money laundering and can furthermore carry encrypted information between criminals. It is argued that NFTs should be regulated according to the object they represent. With regard to supervision and MLFT monitoring this theory is difficult. Particularly because the same type of tokens within the same wallet would be regulated differently. The token for art would have a different legal framework than that representing a piece of (virtual) land. Therefore in relation to MLFT this book suggests that NFTs are supervised by the wallet provider. This will provide a single monitoring framework that is clear for all parties involved.

The next specific challenge with regard to the Metaverse is that of stateless firms. Companies carry the legal nationality of the country that provides them with their legal personality. They need this legal personality in order to obtain basic facilities such as a bank account and the lease of machinery. Within the virtual environment a company can exist without needing such facilities. A legal personality is therefore no longer an absolute requirement. Tracing a virtual company to a physical person or location is furthermore difficult. Stateless firms however can be used to avoid tax, human rights or to launder money. Therefore this book suggests introducing a duty for wallets to verify their corporate customers to physical people. Because whilst each company may differ in their structure they will all require a wallet to receive virtual currency.

In conclusion therefore the current legal framework through the introduction of the AMLD5 has increased its scope to cover virtual currencies. Nevertheless it is not yet fully adept in its response to the Metaverse. Some changes in thinking and definitions are required to create a supervisory framework that reduces the risks of MLFT to an acceptable level. If these changes are not made the Metaverse might become a MLFT paradise.

Open Access This chapter is licensed under the terms of the Creative Commons Attribution 4.0 International License (http://creativecommons.org/licenses/by/4.0/), which permits use, sharing, adaptation, distribution and reproduction in any medium or format, as long as you give appropriate credit to the original author(s) and the source, provide a link to the Creative Commons license and indicate if changes were made.

The images or other third party material in this chapter are included in the chapter's Creative Commons license, unless indicated otherwise in a credit line to the material. If material is not included in the chapter's Creative Commons license and your intended use is not permitted by statutory regulation or exceeds the permitted use, you will need to obtain permission directly from the copyright holder.

SPRINGER NATURE

GPSR Compliance

The European Union's (EU) General Product Safety Regulation (GPSR) is a set of rules that requires consumer products to be safe and our obligations to ensure this.

If you have any concerns about our products, you can contact us on ProductSafety@springernature.com

In case Publisher is established outside the EU, the EU authorized representative is:

Springer Nature Customer Service Center GmbH
Europaplatz 3
69115 Heidelberg, Germany

The manufacturer's authorised representative in the EU is Springer Nature Customer Service Centre GmbH, Europaplatz 3, 69115 Heidelberg, Germany. If you have any concerns regarding our products, please contact ProductSafety@springernature.com

Printed and bound by CPI Group (UK) Ltd, Croydon, CR0 4YY

23/03/2026

02076360-0012